From the author of the
'The Sexual Language (

My Terrifying Shocking Humiliating Amazing Adventures In Online Dating

Ben Arogundade

White Labels Books
LONDON TOWN

My Terrifying, Shocking, Humiliating, Amazing Adventures In Online Dating
First published in 2019 by White Labels Books.
Registered office: 85 Great Portland Street (1st Floor), London W1W 7LT.
www.whitelabelsbooks.com
Copyright ©Ben Arogundade, 2019.

ISBN 978-1-9998351-7-0

Email: enquiries@whitelabelsbooks.com
Twitter: @WhiteLabelsBook
@BArogundade

Written, art directed and designed by Ben Arogundade.
Typeset in Times New Roman.
Cover image by Mike Kemp. ©Mike Kemp/Getty Images.

Printed by KDP.
Available from Amazon.com and other outlets.

Sustainability and environmental consciousness are central to our
ethos. Our books are made-to-order using digital print-on-demand
technology. This means less paper, less waste and reduced transport
and storage costs. Our ink is chlorine-free and our interior paper
stock is supplied by a Forest Stewardship Council-certified provider.
It consists of 30 per cent post-consumer waste recycled material.

This book is dedicated to all those seeking their "one", especially single working mums and women of colour everywhere.

Thank you to all the women I have ever loved, dated or not quite dated. I have learned so much from you.

Apologies to everyone who has ever been my girlfriend, for all the times I was mean, selfish, cruel, judgmental, impatient, dishonest or just a total dick.

Contents

1 Digital Desire   3

2 Why Didn't You Say Something?   13

3 The Spec   33

4 People Of Colour Beware (And Be Aware)   46

5 The Black Women's Guide To Online Dating (The 13 Steps)   64

6 Are All Online Daters Rubbish? (Or Are You The Problem?)   73

7 The Emotional Detective (New Columbo)   85

8 How To Create The Best Online Dating Profile (The 9 Steps)   115

9 The Protocols   137

10 WD-40   158

Dictionary Of Online Dating Terms   176

Acknowledgements   182

1

Digital Desire

I met her the old way, my ex. I was at a charity gala event in London's Park Lane one Sunday evening, and I got seated for dinner at a round table next to her. She had curly black hair, sparkly eyes and a warm smile. We were from very different backgrounds, but we had much in common nonetheless. We talked and laughed for most of the evening, and then exchanged details. She emailed me the next day, and soon after we became boyfriend and girlfriend, for six years. The way it happened was simple and uncontrived, just like millions of other classic boy meets girl scenarios.

I now realise that meeting a partner in this way may never happen to me again.

Instead, I am now an online dater. I would never have admitted that, or written this book even five years ago, such was the stigma around it. It was a mark of shame to admit that in my search for love I had resorted to the seemingly desperate measure of meeting "randoms and crazies" found on the Internet in the same way that one finds items to buy on Amazon. Things are radically different now, as ever greater numbers sign up year-on-year, all concluding the same thing — that there is no other viable option for them to meet someone these days, within the busy, socially isolated lives we all live. For over 60 years since the Second World War, meeting through friends was the most common method for heterosexual couples to meet, but since 2009 this has been in rapid decline. Advancements in digital technology have made this revolution possible, and almost impossible to resist. Over the last decade traditionalists have tried to oppose culture's many digital transformations across music, books, cameras, video and other areas — and failed. History suggests that online dating will also proliferate.

In America this is already a reality. A 2017 survey, *How Couples Meet and Stay Together*, by sociologists at Stanford University and the University of New Mexico, reported that of the romantic partnerships formed in the United States in 2017, 65 per cent of same-sex couples met online, and 39 per cent of heterosexual pairings. These metrics mean that officially, in America, online dating is by far the most common way people now meet. (Statistically, the tipping point happened sometime in 2013). In the UK the figures show the same trend. A 2018 study of 2,000 people by the BBC reported that 45 per cent of 16-34-year-olds had used online dating at some point, and that only 18 per cent of them met their current partner through friends, family or on a blind date.

At the same time as online dating goes up, traditional forms of finding a partner are not only coming down, they are crashing. The American study, which analysed data from 4,000 US adults between 1995 and 2017, presents some sobering statistics about heterosexual couplings:

	1995	2017
Couples who meet through friends	33%	20%
Couples who meet through family	15%	7%
Couples who meet through school	10%	5%
Couples who meet through college	9%	4%
Couples who meet through church	7%	4%
Couples who meet through as co-workers	19%	11%
Couples who meet through neighbours	8%	3%

Judging by this, the writing is very firmly on the wall.

Compelling as the statistics are, perhaps a more telling indicator of the culture shift are the range of professionals now converted to online dating. During my time on the apps I have connected with psychotherapists, doctors and NHS directors, CEOs, scientists, actresses, TV personalities and movie directors, to name a few. These are women with incredible resumes who once upon a time might have had many serious suitors beating a path to their doors — but today no one is knocking, and so willingly and openly, they and others like them, have all signed up. There they all are in plain sight online, and their male equivalents, waiting to be snapped up by anyone who is ready. They are lined up within the apps like commodities, which is exactly what we all are now. The search for relationships has become a branch of online shopping, and horrifying as this may initially seem, it is the reality. Those who resist the tide — the dating Luddites who cling to the nostalgia of courting "the old way" — face hard times ahead. The new thinking is, the wistful, romantic nostalgia for the physical way people used to meet was always misplaced.

Today, fewer single people care about how they meet people — it is the quality of the subsequent relationship that counts.

For those who are actively looking for a partner, the protocols have changed for good. As an old-school guy, once staunchly resistant to online dating, I am now a prime user of its services. As a 52-year-old single male, I live a socially more reduced life than I did in my twenties. My general appetite for going out has diminished, and when I do, I tend to hang out at the same old places with the same old friends, whether there are single women there or not. Also, as a writer, I work alone, with no co-workers and no associated social activities. For me, together with many of Britain's 4.6 million self-employed people, online dating seems the only choice — and within it I have been shocked by what I have discovered. Typically, the older generation have expressed horror at the online dating rituals of the young, shaking their heads judgementally at the morally questionable things they get up to — but now mid-lifers are doing the same things. Mums and dads parade in a state of semi-nudity in their photos; male trolls send illicit messages and "dick pics", while people ghost each other and swipe left on the fat and the ugly. Personally, I have been stood up, ignored, verbally abused, used for sex and asked to be a surrogate father to an unborn child, amongst other things — and all by women in their 40s and 50s. I met two females who had not had boyfriends for 10 years or more, and another who, divorced with kids at 42, had only ever had one relationship in her entire life. I met others who were travelling the world in an effort to avoid finding a man, and yet were signed up to Internet dating in an effort to do just that. I met another who had not had sex for five years, and a married woman who was trapped in a sexless relationship with a man she loved, and was looking for a sexual partner once a week, preferably at his apartment or a hotel.

By far the most prevalent emotional issue I came across amongst divorced women was a mistrust of men. They felt let down or betrayed by their ex-husbands and former partners, and this had made them cynical and wary of anyone new. A number of those I met online assumed and expected that it was only a matter of time before I — as a man — did the same bad thing to them that their ex-partners had done before — whether it was adultery, not supporting them emotionally, or some other issue. I found myself entering into relationships in which, from the outset I was not trusted, because of the actions of men who had gone before me, years prior. I was inheriting the legacy of other men's misdemeanours, like old luggage or hand-me-down clothes. It was as if these women were saying:

Here are some shoes my ex-husband used to wear.
They're yours now.

When I dated females with these views I would do my best to allay their suspicions of me as a member of the opposite sex. "I come armed with kisses, not daggers," I remember saying poetically to one girlfriend. But of course, mere statements of intent are not enough to alter a person's software.

The overall experience online has been more challenging, more shocking and more exciting than anything I experienced dating the old way. That is not to say that digital dating is better, but rather, it is a totally new experience that cannot be compared to its analogue counterpart. Dating the old way you met one person at a time, and always physically, focusing on them and only them, whereas in this revised format you can meet *thousands simultaneously*, all of whom are racked like goods in a vending machine, and none of whom are physical. In the old days, if a date didn't work out, you didn't know where the next was going to come from, or when, but now you do, and this ability to instantly select humans from a menu has altered the nature of the interactions. Now we don't try as hard as we once did, losing the qualities of patience, focus and investigation. We have *lost our sense of resilience.* "Staying power is not in fashion today," says psychotherapist and relationships expert, Esther Perel. "It's not a virtue. It is not a value." We want everything now — not just a partner, but success, money, fame, even entertainment. The popular term, "video-on-demand" is a great example of how this trend currently manifests within contemporary language — and in the same way that we can binge-watch TV dramas on *Netflix*, we can now binge-date, consuming everything in one go in a form of digital gluttony. In eras past we valued the cultural apprenticeship of slow learning, of striving, of trying and failing and learning from it all. But now we complain if we've been online for six months and not met the person of our dreams. Even the way we heal from our break-ups has been modified. Dating digitally now allows us the option of skipping the crucial fallow period between relationships, which we used to use to rest and recover. Instead we can now rebound directly from one to the next without waiting to heal first.

The new rules are also altering the prerogatives of the sexes, socialising us out of the practice of initiating face-to-face verbal approaches. The dating app, *happn* provides a good example. It matches people who live in the immediate vicinity to one another. So, if a man passes a woman on the street whom he likes, he can quickly go to the app to see if she is also present there, as it links those who pass each other. This means there is less incentive for a man to make a direct approach, even when a woman is actually standing right there in front of him. I had a recent conversation with a female friend who is in her late 40s, who confessed to struggling with Internet dating because she still expected and wanted men to approach her the old way, as she had become accustomed to as a woman throughout her adult life. The idea that she, in the post #MeToo arena, might make the first move, was an anathema to her, as no doubt it is for certain other women of her generation. But today, why should a man approach a woman when potentially dozens are approaching him on *Tinder* — and all at once? Some women are finding this new reality hard to accept. In my friend's case she is a white, middle class successful professional who is accustomed to winning in all aspects of her life. But the prospect of suddenly losing at something as fundamental as finding a partner was jarring to everything she knew of herself. Her personality, accomplishments and attractiveness, which had worked seamlessly in attracting males in the past, suddenly stopped working — her prerogatives destroyed by the new dating tech, much in the same way that technology has destroyed other manually-driven cultures throughout history. She had reached a terrifying new moment in life:

I am no longer attracting the best. Shit.

But if white women like my friend think they've got it bad, they should spare a thought for black women. White females sit at the top of the preferences table for women within the online dating pool, whereas black women are firmly at the bottom. Statistically they receive fewer messages, are swiped less and abused more than any other group. While privileged white females can complain about Internet dating's disappointments, and be heard, black women's often more troubling experiences are relegated to the margins.

The changes in the gender roles within online dating make it seem like an invention that was always waiting to happen. For men, having the confidence to approach a woman and to risk rejection and humiliation has always been a problem, while for women the feelings of disempowerment at having to wait for male advances has been a point of frustration. The new rule online is that *everybody approaches everybody simultaneously*. He or she who hangs back waiting, loses. Love online is hyped and accelerated, as if it is no longer love as we traditionally know it, but some new strain — more propulsive, transactional and disposable. It is as if the Darwinian theory of sexual selection has evolved to a more hardcore level.

Aside from levelling the playing field in giving both genders more agency to instigate connections, there are other ways in which online dating may actually work better than the way things were before. People can find out more of the critical details about daters in advance of meeting, which is harder to do if you are being fixed up by friends on a blind date. Online, a person can also block unwanted advances in ways they could not have done before, resulting in many feeling safer online than in the days when they had to meet men in advance of being able to vet them. Online dating also allows you to hone in on personal preferences. People can search according to height, age, ethnicity, politics, occupation, sexual preference, etc. Research also suggests that heterosexual couples who meet online and forge serious relationships transition to marriage more quickly. One reason offered by sociologist Michael

Rosenfeld, who led the Stanford University study, is that the wider choice of partners, and the ability to rapidly glean key information about them, leads to better matches. Selection bias is also a factor — that is, marriage-ready singletons fast-tracking the process by directly choosing each other.

*

My intention in joining the digital dating revolution was not to write this book. I was engaged with the apps because I was genuinely seeking a partner. However, the journey I went on became so fascinating that I felt the need to write something about it. Thus far, most of the books and articles about the subject have been written by young white women — and while their stories have provided very valuable and informative insights into the culture, I didn't see much of my own experience represented — that is, of an older heterosexual man, a black man in his 50s, living in a city (London) in which most of the available women within my age range are white, and divorced with children.

Some of you reading this book may be expecting it to contain lots of juicy stories of my sexual adventures, as it is about online dating after all, which many think is all about sex — but more and more, particularly amongst older singletons, I found their focus to be emotional rather than sexual, and so this text doesn't have very much sex, so if you are reading with that expectation, you should probably stop now. What this story does have however, are many of my observations about human behaviour, as manifested online. The turning point in my understanding of all this, and when I actually began to enjoy online dating, happened when I became what I call an *emotional detective*. By closely analysing the words and imagery within people's profiles I began to make better choices about who to connect with — and who to avoid. Chapter 7 discusses this in detail. My decisions didn't always work, but they was successful in replacing fear with confidence, and even excitement. This is critical, because if online dating is how we all meet now, we have little choice but to embrace it and to learn how to use it safely and effectively.

2

Why Didn't You Say Something?

If you open the pipe, you get sewage. I invented this catchphrase to describe what can happen when you create an online presence in today's crazy world, thereby voluntarily exposing yourself to anyone who wants to word-snipe at you. The phrase has a similar kind of resonance as well-worn standards such as, *If you play with fire, you get burned.* It was with a sense of deep hesitation about being exposed online that I first signed up to some dating apps. I had no idea what to expect, or what to do. Initially I decided to sign up for one month only, and then to take a rest. This was because from the very beginning I didn't like what I was turning into — someone who was constantly checking their phone for messages — but more disturbingly, someone who learned to instantly dismiss human beings with a cursory swipe of a hand, as if they were nothing. We are told to swipe right for attractiveness, and in the other direction for those we don't like the look of, when we all know too well that beauty or attraction alone will not sustain a relationship. What is this mad shit?

As a newbie I initially pored carefully over each woman's online profile, looking at all of their photos and reading all their text from start to finish — that is, when there was text to read. It was an exercise in *slow looking*, which is the way people of my generation were brought up to consume words and pictures.

I began by messaging just one woman. I waited three days. She didn't get back to me. I checked my text message to see if it had gone through. It had. I soon realized what was wrong. I had to swipe or message a lot of them to get one response. In 2018 sociologists from the University of Michigan published research which analysed the messaging habits of 186,000 heterosexual online daters from four US cities — New York, Boston, Chicago, and Seattle. They reported that women only responded to 17 per cent of men's first messages, while men responded to roughly 50 per cent. As soon as I realised how many people there were to get through, and that I needed to up my frequency, I abandoned slow looking, and instead spent less and less time on each one. The longer one spends online, swiping the faces of strangers, the more jaded, or better at assessing candidates, you become, and therefore the faster the flow. I learned to swipe left or right every one or two seconds, like this:

no, no, no, yes, no, no, no, no, no, no, no, yes, no, no, no, no.

A slave to the rhythm, I allowed myself to be brainwashed into dismissing all the humans I didn't find physically attractive, just as I feared when I first signed up. I was easily manipulated into this behaviour by the app's gameified design and slot machine-style graphics. Of course, *Tinder* and the other swipe-based apps did not invent the human propensity to make snap judgements about people based on appearance. Humans have always done this. The selection of a mate has always been this emotionally brutal — but the difference online is that the practice is greatly magnified. Offline, the superficial judgements we make based on aesthetics amount to a small number each day, but within online dating, depending on usage, a person can dismiss *dozens of human beings per day, every day.* This is new, and potentially more frightening than anything we have seen before. What effect does dismissing humans en masse have on how we treat people in real life?

So there I was, at the mercy of online dating tech. Alone, brainwashed, swiping the faces of strangers. How could this stupidity possibly lead to anything meaningful?

*

Splitting up with her was the worst day of my life. Worse than when my mother died. When she passed away it was slow. The cancer took three years to finally get her, and so I could see death coming, and therefore had time to adjust to it — but my break-up wasn't like that. It was swift, sudden and unexpected, and so was therefore much harder to process. She made a formal announcement that it was over, after more than six years. She was crying, but I was not. I was too stunned. I later described the feeling to friends as like being hit by a truck while facing the wrong way in the road. There was no discussion, no exchange of views — she had decided. It was as if, in the rulebook of how to break up, she had torn out the pages of the last chapter — the one in which the end is preceded by the familiar acts of deterioration that couples go through — disagreements, rows, eating meals in silence, sleeping in separate rooms, not having sex, etc. These things were all missing from our end sequence. Everything seemed normal. As far as I was concerned, there were no clear signs of trouble leading up to the event. But of course there were, only

I didn't see them, or I chose not to. Nevertheless, the question that kept ringing in my head was;

Why didn't you say something?

In my subsequent feelings of confusion, sadness and anger, I later came to realise that when people leave in this manner, without trying to resolve issues, it is because their mind is already made up — they are not interested in fixing — they are interested in leaving. Ultimately, the reasons why someone leaves someone else don't really matter, in that they don't change the end result. However, the reasons do matter for the understanding and processing of the person who is being left. But seeking these answers can be difficult, as they will — if they tell the truth — invariably consist of things about you that your ex-partner does not like. So, if you seek "the truth", be sure you can handle it, as the saying goes. In my case, initially I was too shocked by the event itself to insist on hearing her truth. In the moment the bad news hit me, I felt a sudden brittleness in my chest, and I swear my heart broke in two, like someone snapping a biscuit between their thumbs. I thought I would be with her to the end of my life. How can so many of us be so collectively wrong in our assumptions and expectations about how long our relationships will last? We feel like fools in our miscalculation of the longevity of love, and we emerge broken, disappointed and cynical, in absolute contrast to the blissful early period of our romances. *Wow, those early days! What happened to them? What happened to us? When did it turn? When was the moment of the start of our decline?*

In truth, the roots of every decline do not form over time but are there at the outset. On our first date, as we began our love affair, she turned to me and said;

Ben, I don't think you've been loved properly in your life.
I am going to do it.

Now we were splitting up, and this was gone. I heard a loud voice in my head say;

Well, what happened to that promise, huh?

In that moment I felt a kinship with the young, angry Alanis Morisette, and her classic song, *You Oughta Know*, from her 1995 album, *Jagged Little Pill*. She is raging after a bad break-up with her boyfriend, spitting pain about how she feels betrayed by him. She sings;

You told me you'd hold me until you died,
til you died, but you're still alive.

The reality is, love can wear out, or at least cool down, which is why it so often gets compared to a flame. The undying, unconditional love we humans often promise to each other is actually an aspiration rather than a perpetual state of being. Someone can say to someone else, "I will always love you" — but how can they possibly know? One day, they might not.

Over time, instead of being angry about no longer being the subject of someone's unwavering love, I evolved a new, more proactive question for myself;

Ben, forget blaming her, what was
your role in your break-up, arsehole?

At the beginning I did not know the answer to this question —
but that did not matter as much as knowing that I actually had
a role, and therefore accepting some responsibility for events,
instead of putting it all on the other party, as myself and Alanis
had done.

And so in the aftermath, there I was, unexpectedly single
at 52, dazed and unprepared for the scary new world of online
dating, and the rules around how men and women now meet
and connect. The last time I was single *Tinder* did not exist.
In fact, when I first started dating, the Internet did not exist.
Neither did mobile phones, selfies or turmeric lattes. Like many
of you reading this, I belong to a generation who encountered
potential partners exclusively within real life social scenarios,
and where you spoke face-to-face with a three-dimensional
flesh-and-blood human, while looking into their eyes. This
has now almost become a novelty, a quaint anachronism of a
bygone age, like fax machines or vinyl records. *"Wow, you met
someone in a bar? How original? How did you manage that?"*

Despite my concerns, in I went. At the time, like many who
subscribe to online dating, I thought I was ready — although
with hindsight, I was lying to myself. I convinced myself that
I had healed sufficiently, just 10 weeks after my break-up,
and that now was the right time for a new girlfriend — *I am
absolutely ready, yes, yes, absolutely, for sure I am sure, very
sure I am over her, yes, yes, yes, I am sure, so sure, uh-huh.* In
reality I felt hollowed out with insecurity and self-doubt, as if
someone had scooped out my body mass and left me an empty
shell. I realised that by going online I sought to re-boot my
dented self-esteem, to re-validate my sense of self, to attach
to someone that would help me forget, who would ease the
pain, rage and sadness that I felt. I also sought somehow to get

back at her for leaving me. *I am going to go online dating and have sex with lots of amazing women, super spectacular, super, super gorgeous, and then you'll be sorry that you rejected me, when you see who wants me now, ha, ha!*

Soon after signing up women began responding positively to my online profile. There were a range of messages, some saying that I looked young for my age, while others commented on certain photographs they liked. It is amazing how effective a little slice of adoration can be as an emotional antiseptic. Without even meeting any of these unknown admirers, I started to feel slightly better. It didn't matter at that point whether I was attracted to them or not. What mattered was that they were attracted to me — and were telling me so. As messages pinged onto my mobile like little golden prizes, I felt the dopamine rush in my brain. *They want me? They really want me? Oh, so I'm not so bad after all.* This is online dating's biggest secret. We think it exists to help people find partners, but it is more successful as a vehicle to help damaged people recover from their break-ups. More about this later.

At the beginning of my journey with online dating I found the idea of asking a woman out while knowing absolutely nothing about her, and having only seen a blurry headshot of her face, totally ridiculous. This was especially true on *Tinder*, where most of the profiles contain no text at all, just pictures, and so everyone is unknowable. As I scrolled through image after empty image, I wondered:

Why aren't you all saying anything?

I thought again of my ex, who also didn't say anything. I wanted to scream, both at her, and at *Tinder*'s empty profiles.

SPEAK, SPEAK UP! How did we all become so socialised into silence, into self-erasure, into concealing rather than revealing? Online we have learned to express ourselves by saying nothing — silence has truly become golden — and those who do communicate seem only able to do so in *haiku* form, through machines. We all have mobiles now, but we use them for everything except talking. We stare at our screens, our heads cranked downwards, stabbing at the glass with our fingers. The world has become quieter as a result, everybody's engine's silent running. And in the process we have lost a piece of our humanity — and no one seems to mind much.

I soon had my first date lined up. I felt excited on the day. Meeting a new human, a stranger I knew nothing about, someone who could be the woman of my life — or not, was exhilarating. Most of the time though, they turned out not to be, but it didn't take away from that feeling, and the fact that life seemed better on such days.

I met my date at London's South Bank. This is ground zero for the capital's online daters. It is a large, sprawling cultural hub, centrally located, and with numerous bars, cafes and arts venues, all beautifully laid out adjacent to the River Thames. Also, its station, Waterloo, is a major transport intersection, both for those travelling via the Tube and those singletons who live in the commuter belt and venture in via rail. London's other major rail junctions where online daters congregate are Victoria and King's Cross. Cultural and arts venues like this are also good if you are worried about being stood up on a first date. If it happens, then at least you can salvage something of the occasion by going to see some nice paintings instead.

On any given evening or weekend, the foyer bar and café at the South Bank Centre is bustling with first daters you can spot a mile off. On this occasion I was one of them — but my date didn't go well. I didn't fancy her, although I tried to hide it. She didn't look like her online photos — she was older in real life, and wore more make-up. She was smart and chatty, but I also detected a sadness within her, just as there was within me. I tried to appear interested, and nodded appreciatively at everything she said, but my mind was in the past. I was still raw from my break-up, still spinning, not over her, pretending that I was fine, that I was *cool, cool, cool.* It was only when I was actually sitting in front of a new person that I realised how unrepaired I really was.

I was glad when it was over. It was an endurance rather than a pleasure. We stepped out into the street and I said goodbye to her, and she mentioned that she'd had a good time, and I nodded and thanked her for coming out. People often talk about how hard first dates are in those first few seconds when you meet someone that you don't fancy, but it is the leaving that is much harder, when you know you will never see them again, but you somehow pretend you might. I turned away and walked toward the Tube. But as I stared out into the darkness of the night, I was suddenly engulfed in sadness, as memories of my ex came back to me in waves and chopped up episodes. I started to cry as I walked, and I was surprised at myself that it was happening. *Nigerian men don't cry. What the fuck!* My father would have disapproved. He'd have told me to *get strong, stupid fool.* He is dead now, but his legacy lives. As my crying began to intensify I was suddenly aware that someone might see me, and so I wiped my eyes clumsily with the back of my hand and disappeared quickly into the Underground.

My 22-year-old son Zak, is a far more emotionally

connected man than I am or my father was. When I told him the news about my break-up, trying hard not to show how him how broken I was, he was too astute, and he saw right through me, and so he leaned over silently and put his arms around me. Throughout my childhood my father never touched me, never connected with my body except to inflict ritualised violence, and here was my son, filling the void that he could not. It took everything I had not to cry again in the arms of my own child. The whole thing lasted no more than 10 seconds, but it remains to this day the most amazing thing he's done for me.

I took a short break from online dating after that difficult introduction, and soon it was Christmas, the first one without her. I scrolled through the apps again in the run up, thinking that maybe I could arrange some last minute companionship for Christmas Day, but I soon abandoned that emergency idea, as everyone was gone for the holidays, of course. A thought came to me: *What are you doing, trying to get someone for Christmas? Loser. Stay home and eat the pain instead. Eat it with your Christmas Day dinner for one, you lonely fool.*

Christmas passed quietly, but on New Year's Eve I ventured out to my local pub to join in the celebrations. While there I bumped into an old female friend. There'd always been an attraction between us, but nothing had ever happened, as we'd always been in relationships. But on this particular night we were both single, and so we ended up kissing at the back of the pub. It was the first time in over six years that I had tasted someone else's mouth; a fresh aperture, soft and new; her motion a different choreography. All we did that night was kiss, but the electricity of it was all I needed to feel alive again, to feel back in the world.

That night Al Pacino came to me in a dream. It was Pacino

from *Scarface*. He had some specific advice for me. First, he quoted some classic dialogue from the film that anyone who has ever seen it knows well:

In this country, you gotta make the money first.
Then when you get the money, you get the power.
Then when you get the power, then you get the woman.

Pacino then took the same sequence and tailored it to what I was going through with my break-up. He said:

When you break up, you gotta make the healing first.
Then when you get the healing, you get the online dating.
Then when you get the online dating, then you get the woman.

The next morning I decided to take Pacino's advice and get some professional help with my healing. A friend put me in touch with a psychotherapist. This was seen as a total waste of time and money by some of my male friends, particularly the black ones. I find that black people and other ethnic minorities do not generally hold much faith in psychotherapy. They see it as white man's brain medicine. Culturally we were not brought up with it, and the idea that me, the son of Nigerians, was going to go and pay a therapist made them laugh. They thought I'd gone soft. I remember talking to a West African male friend about it, one evening in my local pub.

"So you're going to pay someone to listen to you chat?" he asked, his voice full of disdain.

"Well...yes," I replied.

"To talk?"

"Yes."

"Chatting?"

"Uh-huh."

"And how much is that?"

"…Maybe a hundred pounds an hour."

"What? A hundred pounds an hour? Just to chat? Do you get anything else for that money? Like a meal, or a beer at least?"

"No extras."

"Not even a few snacks? Peanuts?"

"Nope. Just talking."

"Man, you can talk to me for free. My door is always open. Just buy me a pint."

"Thanks for that, but it's not just a chat," I countered. "It's about working through your emotions."

"Man, for that price, I'd rather stay damaged." He was laughing at me now. "What kind of black man are you anyway?" he asked. "You've been brainwashed by the white man. All you need is a good holiday. And you know, for the price of a few of those therapy sessions, you can afford to go away somewhere nice for a week, and just chill."

"Thanks for your support," I replied sarcastically.

I ignored my West African friend's advice and went ahead with the therapy, as planned. What I didn't tell him was that the pain, anger and sadness I felt over my break-up were corroding me from the inside, and that I needed to find some release, rather than to continue holding my feelings in, quietly imploding. Or more accurately, it was not my feelings of pain, anger and sadness that were damaging me, but *my judgement* of her that had led to these emotions. The therapy sessions were amazing in helping me address this. The story of my break-up that I recounted during my first appointment was the same story that most relationship therapists hear. I refer to as *the classic*, because it is so common — you go through a painful split, after which you become afraid to love again, in case you get burned once more, and so you close up and stop trusting. Instead, you self-sabotage — because that is what it is to run from the possibility of love. And in doing so you become one of *the great unrepaired* of our time — pretending to be ready to love, when actually you are not. These classic, fear-based stories of pain feel special to us because they happened to us, but in fact they are not. What happened to me and to you has happened to others before us, and will happen to others in the future, and in exactly the same way. Life is one story, or a set of stories, retold. We are, as humans, *all connected by the sameness of the things we go through,* rather than our differences.

When my sessions finally ended, my therapist turned to me and said something about being rejected by my ex that I will never forget:

> *Do not let the opinion of someone who has hurt you deeply, diminish your sense of yourself.*

The power of her words opened something within me, and I began to cry right there in the room, because that was exactly what I had done to myself after my break-up. Mired in self-doubt, I had allowed myself to be reduced, to become *less than*, as opposed to *more than*.

This same sense of feeling diminished, and therefore detached from one's true self, was something I began to see everywhere within the online dating ecosystem. I remember a first date I went on in a bar near Victoria station. The woman was divorced, and it had been some time since she had been with anyone, and her view of herself had withered after her husband had left her for someone else some years prior. On the outside she seemed confident, but this cloaked an inner sadness I felt in her, similar to my own. She was like a flower transmuted into a closed fist, trying to blossom again, to unfurl. Soon after we sat down to drinks, she asked, "So, what are you looking for? In terms of a relationship, I mean?"

"An 18-carat love affair," I quipped.

"Wow, that's serious gold."

"For sure. I call it emotional bling." We laughed.

Then she asked, "Do you mind if I feel your neck?"

"What?"

"Can I feel your neck? I have a thing about men's necks. The thickness of them."

"Really?"

"Yeah. I don't know why."

I stared at her silently, wondering about her strange request. After a few seconds I said that I didn't mind, and so she took one hand and wrapped it around my neck and squeezed gently. "It's like a miniature tree trunk," she said, smiling. I nodded as if everything made complete sense, then I took her hand from my neck and motioned to kiss her, and her mouth opened but did not move with mine. It seemed to be locked. It was as if, over time, she had become detached her from her sexuality, numbed to the kinetics of sex. I wondered, *is it possible for a sexuality to atrophy through neglect or trauma?* I kissed her again, this time with greater energy, thinking that I might wake something, but still her mouth did not soften. I tried a joke; "Why aren't you moving your mouth? Is your jaw broken?"

We didn't see each other again. We had been drawn together

by our mutual dysfunction, and so the beginning and end of our connection, all of which took place on the same night, was somehow all we needed at the time to feel a little more normal.

Two years after my break-up I had a similar experience with another online dater, this time a 45-year-old divorcee with two young children. She was tall, lean and beautiful, built like a swimmer, with square shoulders and with piercing eyes. Her marriage had ended five years earlier when her ex-husband had an affair with a woman half her age, and this had destroyed her self-esteem, filling her with doubt and shame, and detaching her from true self. *How can a woman so physically beautiful forget what she is*, I thought, as I learned of her plight. I told her she had amazing eyes, and she replied that it was the first time any man had mentioned it. I stared at her with bemusement, because to me it was so obvious. "How can any man have missed that?" I asked. "Where have you been? Prison?"

When we finally had sex, and I scanned her body for the first time, she suddenly became self-conscious and covered her small breasts with both hands. "That's all I've got, I'm afraid," she said apologetically.

I gently moved her arms away. "What's wrong with you?" I whispered. "Kate Moss has got smaller breasts than you, and she's done alright."

I realised again that everybody is damaged in this online dating merry-go-round, particularly us mid-lifers, with our nasty divorces and shattered expectations. There is always a compelling story, even with those who may not be yours or my match. It is the diversity of character one encounters that can be most startling. I once asked a woman out on a date on the first text message I sent after we were matched. She said yes immediately, and off we went. But, on another occasion, when I attempted the same thing with a different woman, she was offended by the very suggestion that we meet up so quickly, without first exchanging some banter. I wondered what experiences had shaped both these women's contrasting reactions. What people had they met in their lives who had influenced their personalities in this way? The experience reaffirmed to me how diverse and unknowable human beings can be, and how things can therefore often go wrong.

I once met a woman on a date who ran a successful catering business employing 50 people. She was divorced with a young child, and had been single for two years. We met at a pub in North London, and the conversation flowed very well. We talked about our respective childhood struggles, our break-ups, and all manner of subjects. Later on I suggested we change venues and have a drink at another pub close by. As we came out into the street, a young girl wearing a white floral-patterned dress passed by simultaneously. I struck up a brief conversation with her as we walked, and I mentioned what a great dress it was, and how beautiful the pattern was. She then branched off, and we went our separate ways. But as I walked away toward the pub with my date, something happened:

"Why did you talk to that girl?" she asked.

"What?"

"Why did you talk to her?"

I was surprised by her question, and took a few seconds to respond. "Er...what do you mean?"

"Why did you start talking to her? You don't even know her."

"Er...well, I saw her dress and the pattern, and so I spontaneously thought I'd communicate. It was a nice design, and I have an eye for graphics. There was nothing sinister in it,

I was merely making conversation."

"But, she was upset by it."

I frowned. "What? No, she wasn't."

"She was. She was blushing."

"That doesn't mean she was upset. That's your interpretation. You have no idea how she felt."

"That's true," she conceded finally.

There was a silence as we walked. The incident had triggered something within her. I did not know what, but things were broken now.

"Listen, I'm going to cancel that drink," she said finally.

"Oh...OK...well..."

"I'm going to go."

"Right...OK, well, you do what you need to do."

"OK, bye."

And with that, she was gone. In a single moment, a date that had been going well, crashed.

As a result of experiences like this I came to believe that there is no such thing as a "bad date". We are all the sum total of every experience we have ever had with those we have met, however fleetingly. We are defined, nourished and also damaged by these interactions, as every encounter adds to our personal data bank, deepening our knowledge and experience. As someone who works alone, human connections are something I crave each day, as a writer, as a Londoner and as a human being, regardless of the age or gender of the person I am connecting with, or whether or not they are strangers. In this regard I would rather be out on a date that went wrong, like this one, than sitting home alone with a TV dinner on my lap. There is always a chance that, far from being what we call "a waste of time", these interactions may enlighten us in some way, or in this case end up being put to good use as a passage in this book. I found being single easier to bear when I was actively meeting new people, not even necessarily for romance, but to go beyond romance in seeking out and listening to their stories, and hearing about the things they were going through. Many online daters stipulate categorically that they are looking for romance only, and not "coffee hook-ups", or friendships. This suggests that having friends is a closed loop, with no possibility of new entrants. I disagree with this approach. I have many friends, but there is always room for more if they are amazing people. Why would I not say yes to the opportunity to meet a fantastic new person who might enrich my life even further? But then again, as a writer, this viewpoint may be expected, as so much of life's experience ends up being editorial material. I am also aware that all this may be a very male perspective. For many women, the experience of dating men is often more unpleasant, if not traumatic, because many of them behave badly, and also women may not always feel safe in their company.

By the end of my eventful introduction to online dating, I had changed my mind about the stupidity of the practice of swiping humans left or right — or more accurately, I came to the conclusion that persisting with this mechanism was worthwhile, due to the incredible diversity of people I was meeting, and that I would never have met without the Internet.

Six reasons why women swipe left on me:

1. They think I am a playa.
2. They don't fancy me.
3. They don't fancy black men (or are suspicious of them).
4. I am too old.
5. I already have children.
6. I am only looking for Londoners, and they live elsewhere.

3

The Spec

Many online daters believe that the key to finding the right partner is to be as broad as possible in the scope of their searches. This is incorrect. Because there are so many people to choose from online, narrowing the field, as opposed to being open, is critical. It is about *elimination rather than accumulation.* When I began Internet dating I had no clear idea about the woman I was looking for. If I'd been asked then, I would have said something vague like, "Someone nice" — a non-descript term rather than a precise specification. Think about it like this: if you were going to buy a new car, you wouldn't simply purchase any vehicle so long it was "nice". You might seek one that had good fuel consumption, or was electric, or had generous legroom, or four doors, etc. This is a spec. Crude as my analogy is, the principle is obvious. Anyone who does not have a clear idea of the exact spec of partner they are looking for will struggle with online dating. Sites like *Hinge*, *Bumble* and *Guardian Soulmates* do part of the job for you by making you fill in a questionnaire of preferences when you sign up, but you should still have your own ideas. I am continually amazed at how many smart people with well-organised lives have no idea what kind of partner they seek. I once went on a date with a top executive in the movie business who was like this. A while after we sat down, I asked her if she was looking for a boyfriend.

"I don't know," she replied after some thought.

"What do you mean, you don't know?" I countered. "You are Internet dating. Surely…"

"I know…but I haven't really thought about what I want, to be honest."

Her answers surprised me, but then I remembered that I was once in the same emotional position. Not knowing my own spec was a sign that I was not ready for a new relationship, and I detected that the same was true of her. When a person first becomes single, the thing they often feel most is not the desire for sex, or the need to have a new partner — it is loneliness. The desire to connect with someone is more important than having a clear idea of who the person may be. They key factor is to be listened to, and heard. Even the comfort of a stranger can provide some emotional uplift. I remember the feel-good factor of arriving home from work, and while making supper for one, getting a ping on my phone from someone. Suddenly in that moment I felt wanted, and a little less lonely. Despite the fact that the person may not even turn out to be what I want does not detract from the excitement of the moment, or the sense of anticipation of the date itself.

As time went on, by trial and error I managed to hone down my own preferences. By the end, my ideal spec of woman read like this:

Mental state: Emotionally available.
Location: London (and its immediate radius).
Kids: Don't mind, but if she has them, teenagers ideal.
Age: 40 to 55.
Height: 5'5 to 6'1.

Body: Slim or athletic.
Exercise: Yes.
Religion: Any, but no atheists.
Profession: Creative/media.
Education: University level.
Pastimes: nature, the arts, fine food, restaurants, pubs, Radio 4.
Politics: Liberal.
Dress sense: Stylish/fashion conscious.
Pets: Don't mind.
Food: Healthy.
Smoking: No.
Alcohol: Yes.
Ethnicity: Any.

In many ways reducing ones search to a summary of requirements like this is disturbing because it is a list, as if we are going shopping — but actually we are — we are online shopping for a human being; one to share our lives with. There is no getting away from this unsettling fact. The big difference here is, when you shop for someone who you may then decide you don't want after opening the package, it's harder to send them back.

But at best all specs are wish lists. In reality we seldom meet anyone who has the whole set, but daters should always aim to get as close as they can. For example, within my spec I have noted that I am not into atheists. As a spiritual person, I believe there is a force beyond this life, and so having a partner who was completely closed to having that conversation would be difficult.

ACTION:
If you don't know your spec, write one before you create your online profile. It will help you create a clear picture in your mind of the person you are looking for. Use my headings above as a guide.

But even when you have refined your spec, it will be meaningless unless it is coupled with a healthy dose of sexual attraction and chemistry. The unknowable, unpredictable nature of this element makes it the one elusive component no one can list or quantify within a spec. It is *Factor X*. Discovering that you and your potential partner do not have it, may instantly disqualify the partnership, even if they tick every other box within your carefully designed spec. This is one of the hardest things about online dating — not feeling that sexual spark with great people with fantastic personalities and resumes. You know that you should fancy them, and you really want to — but you don't. You just don't.

My own spec was developed on the back of lifestyle preferences and different experiences gleaned while dating. As a man over 50, my archetype is very clear — a well-preserved woman in her 40s or early 50s, who is into yoga, Radio 4 and 6 Music, country walks, wine and cheese. She's also probably divorced with kids. I found that the women who fitted this spec were not looking for a partner in the conventional sense. They already had established lives, careers, houses, cars, etc. They were not seeking a father figure for their children, or even for me to necessarily move in with them. They were looking for a *companion rather than a provider*. To break it down, they actually wanted three things:

1. Quality chat.
2. Emotional presence.
3. Some proper sex.

In principle this "Big 3" is a much simpler set of deliverables than is required of young daters, who have the added complications of the fact that they have yet to be married, have kids, a big job or a mortgage. In this case, a woman is more typically looking for a companion *and* a provider, or co-provider. But despite the middle-aged man's reduced role, many struggle to supply the Big 3 — in other words, to be in a partnership in which they are not bringing and holding the economic power. With this gone, it only leaves the relationship as the standalone requirement, and many men are unrehearsed in this revised role.

Of course, some men of my age who are divorced with kids, opt for a woman in her thirties, or even younger, who has no children and has never been married. I have a friend who went in this direction. His reasons were that he thought these women were easier to be with because they were childless, with more free time, were physically and aesthetically in better shape, and free of the cynicism and emotional wounding divorced people often harbour. But these relationships that appear easier on paper, are not. The age gap can cause problems in terms of where both parties are within their life development, and the woman may one day want her own children — and possibly not with a much older man who already has kids of his own.

As for some of the other items on my spec list, in terms of the ethnicity of my potential partner, in my opinion true love is hard enough to find online without restricting myself to a specific ethnic group, and so I will take love in whatever form

I find it, whatever the colour of the packaging. Also, in terms of physical fitness, I exercise regularly and also eat healthily, and so I would prefer someone who mirrors this, and whose body type reflects this lifestyle too. *Guardian Soulmates* includes a category for users to describe their preferred body type. There are three options — slim, athletic or average. Shallow as it may seem, whenever I read someone's profile in which they described themselves as "average", I found myself not clicking through. The word bothered me. I don't want average anything. I want excellent, I want amazing.

My spec is also welcomes pet-lovers. I find that this generation of single women are obsessed with animals, particularly dogs. I have never seen so many images of online daters cuddling their pooches. There are as many dogs within dating profiles as there are people. I sometimes wonder what these women want a boyfriend for when their relationships with their pets seems so intimate and fulfilling. I remember reading one profile in which a woman wrote, "If you don't love my dog, you can't love me." I thought, *Really?* Why can't I just *like* your dog? Why does it have to be love? Many women view their pets with an equal level of importance as mothers with children. They are an integral part of the household, and if the new boyfriend does not adapt, he won't last. And part of that adaptation may mean taking it for walks, picking up poop and potentially sleeping three-in-a-bed with little Scooby.

Of all the items within my spec, for the over 40 the most critical consideration in evaluating a potential new partner is *availability and logistics*, or A&L, as I call it. Availability refers to how much time a person actually has within their busy life to devote to being someone's girlfriend or boyfriend, while logistics refers to how you make being together actually happen. For the mid-lifers, A&L matters more to a relationship's success than being cute, intelligent, funny or sexy. If there was such a thing as an A&L questionnaire, it would include questions like this:

How much availability do you have to be in a relationship?
How far away do you live? Who will do the travelling?
How much will it cost to get there and back?
Will we see each other during the week, or is it just weekends?
How old are your children?
How much time off do you have from them?
Will I have a surrogate role to play with your kids?
How tricky is your ex, and will I have to deal with the motherfucker?

This approach at first seems cold and unromantic, but then, so is swiping the faces of strangers on a phone. Love begins with making pragmatic choices that the apps ask for when you sign up. Romance is phase two, if we're lucky.

Older women with the most sought after A&Ls are those without children, or whose kids have grown up and left home. With no childcare responsibilities they are free evenings and weekends for a full-blown relationship, and are mobile enough to travel. I was once contacted by a single woman in her 40s, who wrote in the first line of her profile that she had three young children and two dogs — and I must admit, straight away I felt exhausted by this intro, compared to the *lightness* of a woman alone. Childless single women currently present a small, although sought after fraction of the over 40s online dating pool, but this demographic is rising rapidly. Almost everywhere in the world, the more that women achieve educationally, the higher the proportion that remain childless. This has shifted from one-in-10 of those born in 1946, to one-in-five of those born in 1970. In Germany 22 per cent of women now reach their early 40s without children. The highest rates of childlessness occur amongst females who pursue degrees in non-vocational subjects. Researchers at Stockholm University report that 33 per cent of Swedish women born in the late 1950s, and who studied social sciences, did not have children, compared with 10 per cent of primary-school teachers.

In the online world these women are providing stiff competition for other females within the dating arena, where most of the candidates are typically divorced with children, with many living out of town, and also juggling demanding jobs. A&L is a massive issue for those in this category. If, for example, a man dates a woman with kids, and she lives in the same town, getting to see her can be a simple matter of a short journey. This suggests an increased A&L, as you can potentially see the person during weekday evenings as well as weekends. If by contrast a man dates someone who lives in another town, they may only get to see them at weekends — and if, according to the "standard arrangement", the children spend alternate weekends with their father, that means, in terms of actual time spent alone together, the couple will only have two weekends a month — or *four days out of 30*. And this assumes that the couple spend all that time together, and not partially with family or friends during those weekends off, which is more likely. If they spend some time elsewhere, it will actually amount to less than four days a month. This basic math reveals how difficult such relationships are. The ultimate solution is for the couple to live together, but this may not be practical or desirable, and if it is, it certainly won't happen in

40

the early period. Many people, in their enthusiasm for dating someone they like, dive into relationships like this without considering the A&L — and then after the honeymoon period the relationship struggles.

For busy, stressed, single parents, time together with a partner often occurs in snatched moments which happen away from the home or the bedroom. Some of my most memorable and intimate times have happened while on public transport or in supermarkets. They are sometimes the only places where you can be alone together, even though in reality you are anything but that. I recall one relationship that revolved around weeknights after work, when I would meet her at Victoria Station, and we would catch the train to her house in Surrey. We would kiss and hold hands as we sat next to each other, hoping the journey wouldn't end. But as soon as it did we would crash back into reality — into her house full of demanding children who needed to be listened to, fed and put to bed, and suddenly our time together would come to an abrupt halt — until the train back into London the next morning. I learned to appreciate these fragments of time. An hour uninterrupted was a treasure. A whole day, a luxury.

Out-of-town single working mums with young kids are one of the most difficult categories within online dating. In terms of finding a partner, they get the shit sandwich. For them, living in commuter belt towns — the twilight zones that city-based men don't want to go to — means fewer choices for them locally within the dating pool. This forces them to look further afield, seeking out those in the big city, but these men may not want to travel outwards, especially if they have local options. Sometimes the distances are bigger than the commuter belt. Despite the fact that I live in London, and made it clear in my profile that I preferred someone local, I was once contacted by a woman in Aberdeenshire, Scotland. Note the word, "shire" here. This means she lived out in the countryside, beyond the city. There was no way I could just pop up there for a coconut cappuccino, and then get the Tube back. For single mums like this, making a beeline for a man who lives so far away is a long shot, but for them, there are very few local options.

Sometimes the enquiries come in from abroad. I once received a message on *Tinder* from a 41-year-old with Kim Kardashian-style curves. This chat went like this:

"Hi, thanks for connecting," I wrote. "Do you mind if I ask, your profile says you are currently 15,160 kilometres away. Are you on holiday?"

"No, I live in Australia," she replied. "I thought it was a good idea to try and expand my horizons."

"Really? But how do you see us meeting up? You're not exactly around the corner."

"Alright then. Good luck."

And that was that. I wondered if she was really looking for a boyfriend. Perhaps she was just lonely, and wanted someone to talk to? Or maybe, like me in my first online moves, she was using dating apps, not to find love, but to revalidate herself?

Another disadvantage for older single woman is that when they separate from or divorce their partners, their decision to have custody of the children can be both the best decision for them, but the worst decision for their dating life. While the ex-husband benefits from not having the children live with him, allowing him to skip happily away and date or remarry someone new without restriction, the woman's ability to move on with a new man is restricted, as she has less availability as primary child carer, and some single men are put off by this.

To further compound the problem, many male singles favour females with teenage children, or none at all, and balk at the prospect of potentially caring for someone else's youngsters in their free time, alongside any they may have themselves. In the fairest divorce arrangements custody is shared 50-50, rendering both parties with the same amount of free time to potentially put into a new partner, but there does not appear to be many of these scenarios in today's settlements.

For single mums, this is how the differing age groups of their children are viewed by men within online dating:

1. Very young kids
Full-on childcare for the next decade, very limited availability to date. Possible surrogate father duties too.
Degree of difficulty — high.

2. Young kids
Full-on childcare for the next five years, but still limited availability to date. Possible surrogate father duties.
Degree of difficulty — medium.

3. Teenagers
No more childcare issues, no surrogate father duties, and she is free for dinner, chat and proper sex any night. (Yay!)
Degree of difficulty — low.

On top of this, the harsh reality for women with young or very young children, and the busy lives they live, is that there is actually very little time left for the relationship they seek and deserve. Work takes up much of their energy, and so they are perpetually exhausted. Weekday nights are awkward for seeing a boyfriend because, by the time they are home from work and they've sorted out the kids and got them to bed, it is 8 or 9pm, after which there is barely time to eat before crashing out themselves. For the ones with these circumstances who live out of town, and are dating men from London, the chances of seeing them during the week for what I call *the mid-week dash* — dinner, chat and sex — are slim. And then, for these single mums, at the end of the week, when the kids go to bed, they are exhausted, and ready for nothing else but to fall asleep with a glass of wine in front of *Netflix*. Then there are the weekends, which perpetually revolve around catching up on sleep and catering to the children's needs — which invariably means ferrying them to play dates, parties or to play sports.

This pattern goes on for years and years, until the kids become independent teens, and their mothers are suddenly *free, free, free*. But what man wants to wait around for five or 10 years before he finally gets to be alone with his partner — as well as all the other difficulties mentioned? Before Internet dating, a man would invest his energy in a woman in this situation, but now he has lots of other options to choose from. A city-based single man, when assessing an out-of-towner, will ask himself questions like: *Why should I venture out to some boring small town where they don't even have good coffee, when I can go local? Or; Why should I choose a woman with screaming young bratty kids, when I can choose one with no kids?* The overwhelming volume of choices means everyone, men and women, get picky, whereas in the days before online dating, we were braver and less harsh.

All these factors conspire in pushing single mums into one of online dating's most difficult categories, when all they have done is love their children, work hard, and not live in the city.

ACTION

The first thing for women in this situation to do, is know your competition. A single woman with young children, and who lives out of town, is competing directly with a woman who lives in the city, who either does not have kids, or else has teenage or grown-up kids. Even if you both live in the city, you are still at a dating disadvantage in terms of having young children. So, how can you compete with this spec? Firstly, in your profile, or your subsequent text exchange, state your A&L. Be open and clear about how much time you actually have for the relationship you seek. Why? Because your competitor has more time for the relationship, and so in order to compete, you need to carve out space too. If you do not have the time, consider asking yourself if you are at the right place in your life to have a relationship.

Secondly, have better pictures than your competitor. Instead of uploading a bunch of sloppy, blurry selfies, create good quality shots that make your profile stand out. Include a well-written profile too. Make it sparkle, and ensure there are no typos, or bad clichés (like how much you love Netflix, cheese, wine or a good chat). Most men may not read your lovely words, but some will. Remember, the more a man likes you, the more he will be prepared to travel, and to engage with your gorgeous young kids. (See chapter 8 for tips on how to create an amazing profile).

A word of warning — these strategies could still fail. If you try them to the best of your ability, and they crash, you may simply have to accept that things will not turn until your children are independent teens, and your availability increases, thereby affording you more energy to capture your partner.

4

People Of Colour Beware (And Be Aware)

If you are the person that loves dancing, walk hand in hand,
cinema and you are a romantic man!
Is definitely a match!

PS: Black men are welcome.

This is the text of a real *Tinder* profile of a 53-year-old white woman, 5'8', educated, no children. She went on to describe her dream dinner guest as Idris Elba, the British actor. Elba's name comes up a lot amongst UK online daters, as the black man whom white women most want to sleep with. I had a conversation about him with a woman I met on *Hinge*, that went like this:

"Black men are sexier than white men," she said.

"Really?'

"Of course. It's true. Put it this way — who would you rather sleep with — a Bill-Gates-looking nerdy white man — or Idris Elba?"

"Actually, neither of them," I replied. "I'm not into men. Not even the black ones."

"Oh, you know what I mean."

"Just because Idris looks like he can fuck better than Bill Gates, doesn't mean he can. Bill could be a secret demon in bed, you don't know."

"I'll take my chances with Idris, thanks."

She was a divorced Englishwoman who had never dated a black man before, but now, in her post-divorce, refurbished self, she said she was "trying something new" by connecting with me. *Trying something new — what am I, a salad? A new strain of broccoli?*

Now that online dating makes it easy to find anyone you want, sex with a black man has become something that a certain group of divorced white women now put on their bucket lists, alongside other post-divorce "experiences" — trekking in Nepal; *check*. Visiting the Northern Lights; *check*. Volunteering to help impoverished children in Africa; *check*. Zip-lining in Costa Rica; *check*. Crazy sex with a black man; *check, check, check!* Soon black people will be competing with ultra-experiences, like a visit to the moon on Virgin Intergalactic.

On another occasion I matched with a white divorcee on *Bumble* who was also seeking "experiences". She lived in the commuter belt outside London. For our first date she took the train into Victoria station, and we met at South Kensington Tube. She was tall and beautiful, and wore a full-length red shirt-dress and pumps. We went to a wine bar adjacent to the station, and I ordered us two glasses of red. As we settled down, I asked her why she'd messaged me.

"You looked fit, and I thought you were a playa," she boldly replied.

"Really? But...I didn't say I was a playa in my profile."

"I just assumed you were."

"Why?"

"...I don't know."

"Because a black man must be a playa, right? He can't be into the relationship, only sex?"

"Well...that's what I thought, I suppose. I've only ever slept with white men, and after my divorce I just wanted to have some fun, to do something different. So I saw you, and I thought you'd have a better body than a white man, better than my ex — and I did think you were a playa, and so you wouldn't be after a relationship."

At that moment I heard a voice in my head: *What the fuck is this beautiful idiot saying?* I was annoyed that a white woman in her position would not consider a black man like me a viable relationship candidate. As she spoke I realised that to her, a black man is *a fucker, not a father. Good for fucking, but not family*. And of course, a promiscuous person is also by definition, untrustworthy. So often we are seen as "half-men" by many on the online dating scene — "drifters" who can only be relied upon for one thing, and this characterisation often synchronises with women who are in emotional transition after their break-ups, and are therefore only looking for "a bit of fun". But then after the fun's over, the implication is that a white woman would return to a white man for the real relationship. Except, this ideal does not actually hold true these days, because if it did, they would be no divorced white women online dating, whereas instead there are thousands, all divorced from their white men. It just goes to show, it is the character of the man that matters most, not the colour.

In response to my date's comments I jokingly pointed out the racism implicit within her assumptions — and I say "jokingly" because this is the only reaction that works, in terms of challenging such views. Anger doesn't play well on a first date — and besides, "angry black man" is yet another stereotype we are already dealing with. I felt a sense of duty to inform, as the first black man she had ever dated. Her real life opinions about black people were hanging on my conduct. Using humour also meant that she felt less judged and threatened, and so was more candid about her prejudices. She felt comfortable enough to tell me that there was no doubt in her mind that black men were biologically and sexually different to whites. She had no idea that this was the same theory once put forward by white physicians during the era of so-called "race science" in seventeenth century Europe.

In most cases that I encountered these ideas, it was the first time the white women in question had ever considered that they might harbour unconscious racist views. Although they all either lived or worked in London, the world's most multicultural city, almost everyone in their lives were white, and so their assumptions about race had never been challenged, until now. What was shocking was the extent to which intelligent women such as these were simultaneously unintelligent about cultural life outside of white values. I recall meeting one woman whose entire frame of reference for her prejudices about blacks were based on what she had seen on television and YouTube.

With these stereotypes and misconceptions about me still shaping many white women's interactions with me, I fantasized about being able to re-frame the way the world sees me as an entity — and the online dating world also. This would be my new order:

1. A being.
2. A human being.
3. A man.

4. A black man.

Instead, society presently sees me in the *opposite* order, which is why racism and discrimination still proliferate — and herein lies the problem with us all — we see *the what*, before we see *the who*. Within online dating, with its top-heavy focus on image, I am often judged first as black man, and sometimes only as that. This makes having a written accompaniment within my profile all the more important, in order to say more about who I am, rather than less. To not do so invites the possibility for white people to judge me solely along racially stereotypical lines — as playboy, stud, drug dealer, criminal, animal, etc. Some may argue that this strategy won't make any difference, as daters generally do not read written profiles anyway, but some do. Moreover, even if no one ever reads a word a black person writes, they should still write the profile, because it illustrates *what you think of yourself.* You may believe that no one is looking at your written summary, but you are.

I must point out that there were also many white women who contacted me referencing things I had written in my profile, without seeming to be motivated by the aforementioned stereotypes, except out of intellectual curiosity. However, being perceived sexually by some affected the kinds of photographs featured within my dating bio. I made a decision to downplay "the playa" stereotype by never showing my body — no bare-chested mirror selfies in the gym, or semi-nudity of any kind. I didn't want to encourage any women to think I was just *fantasy fuck-meat.* I wouldn't have minded being fuck-meat back in my early twenties, when a man is happy that lots of women want him for sex — but at 52 I was looking for companionship and love, and so suddenly I found this idea offensive. There is little appeal for me these days in women thinking of me simply as a hyper-masculine, hydraulic appendage. I wanted someone who was interested in *character before colour*.

My inner voice offered another perspective: *Black men like you are too serious, too intense — all this crap about character! What's wrong with lots of white women wanting to fuck you? It's worked for Mick Jagger.*

On one occasion, on *Tinder* a white woman pinged me her profile, which consisted of a close-up image of her naked backside lying on a bed, wearing only a G-string. There were no other images, no text, no name — just a visually dismembered section of her body, objectified by its owner. What was I to make of this? Was it a fake profile? I swiped left and moved on. That's what I do now that I am 52-years-old, and with a different outlook on life. But 25 years ago? I would have investigated the opportunity, for sure.

Online dating is very effective at revealing how stereotypes about the sexuality of people of African descent are still very much alive and kicking. The concept of *black sex, or African sex* — the assertion that members of this ethnic group are sexually and biologically different from whites, and with a more developed sexuality, dates back to the colonial era. In the 1600s, as the English first began exploring Africa, they focused on the sexuality of the locals, as they often wore no clothes, many tribes were polygamous, and their matrimonial practices differed from those of Christians — all of which European travellers found provocative, if not uncivilised. In 1623 English sea captain and trader Richard Jobson, stated in his journal that the African males he'd observed were "furnished with such members as are after a short while burthensome unto them." He went on to claim that African penises were so large as to rupture unborn foetuses.

And so the stereotype was born.

Jobson's comments sparked off the next four centuries of writings and rumour that black men were well endowed. This went hand-in-hand with the assertion that Africans possessed a more libidinous nature than whites, and which rendered them more animal than human. Even before Jobson's writing, this idea was already established within English popular culture. For example, in Shakespeare's *Othello* (1604), the villainous Iago's campaign of defamation against the Moor makes use of this animalistic imagery, likening his coupling with Desdemona to mating with "a Barbary horse".

Within the dating sphere remnants of Britain's colonial past continue to resonate, only now in digital form. The idea that sex with a black person will yield a more heightened experience from that with a white person continues to drive many hook-ups and one-night-stands on *Tinder*. I was once "jokingly" told by a woman I dated that her white friends were eagerly waiting for her to report back to them about what a black man was like in bed. The implied promise is that the sex will be wilder, the orgasms more intense, more animal, more *crazy, crazy* — closer to what is known as, a "jungle fuck" — because of course, the jungle, within the white imagination, is where many think blacks are from, and a jungle fuck is better than other prevailing varieties. Black writer Stephanie Yeboah came up against these sexual stereotypes during her time online dating. "Some blatantly exclaim that they would want to be in a relationship [with me] to 'get a taste of jungle fever' and to see whether black women are 'as aggressive in bed as they've heard'," she told *The Independent* in August 2018.

When it comes to sex, or indeed life in general for that matter, black men are not free to be as mediocre as white men are privileged to be. They have always had to be that much better to be accepted. On April 15, 1947, when Jackie Robinson became the first African American baseball player to make it into the major league, he had to be that much more talented than his white counterparts. The same was true of Barack Obama when he was elected US President in 2008 and 2012. There has always been a prevailing sense that a white man can be of average ability and rise all the way to the top in life, but a black man has to be excellent at everything — even sex, or so it seems online. When a white woman sleeps with a black man for the first time, she is not expecting the same sex she would get from a white man — she is expecting *next level sex*, as she is fully aware of the stereotype. For the black man, this is not sex as we know it, as an act of pleasure — it is *pressure sex* — sex as performance art, defined by race.

But what if you are a black person who just has sex like a normal human, in a non-jungle-fucky-like way? The implication is that this will be a disappointment to the white woman (and her friends) who expected the opposite. You can just hear it now; *Yeah, I slept with a black bloke once. It was rubbish.* In fact, when a black man is faced with the prospect of sex with a white woman for the first time, there are only three ways it can play out:

1. Badly — thereby killing the stereotype.
2. Averagely — thereby proving that a black man is just a regular guy with regular skills.
3. Amazingly well — thereby perpetuating the white man's stereotype.

Which of these three should a black man deliver — or more accurately, can he deliver, and consistently? The future of sexual politics and racial stereotypes is riding on it. In my case, so disappointed was I about the sexual stereotype assigned to me, that on one occasion with a white woman I met online and slept with, I deliberately tried to make the sex mediocre. I wanted to smash the stereotype. I wanted sex to be normalised, finally, like it is for white men.

For certain black men who play on the stereotype, sex has become a way for them to outwit white males, to subvert the patriarchal control they have lived under since slavery and the colonial era, and still live under today. Context is important here, because black online daters are operating within a network of apps created and controlled predominantly by white men. We struggle to escape what many black writers, from W.E.B. Du Bois to Toni Morrison, have referred to over the decades as, *the white gaze* — that black people exist within a biased societal framework created and controlled by white patriarchy, and which places all others in a position of inferiority. The "eye" of the white gaze is suspicious, patronising, denigrating, discriminating. It is the eye that killed Trayvon Martin, the 17-year-old African American youth shot dead by a neighbourhood watch volunteer, who was then acquitted. Within the criminal justice system, healthcare, education, housing, jobs — and now within Internet dating, blacks are less than equals with whites. But this particular white gaze presents a different strand, a new mutation — the *digital white gaze* of online dating is one black people volunteer for. We enter the room willingly, offering up our often semi-naked bodies, but this time the gaze is invisible, consisting of white people we can't see, looking at us, judging us through their screens.

But it is important for black people not to allow themselves to be defined by this presence, or to give in to its fear-based narrative. We have to transcend who we think is watching, and instead focus on how aspects of it might actually work for us. Equally, it would be wrong to view the digital white gaze as totally malevolent. Through its invisible gauze I have been contacted by some amazing, inspirational white women, fearless, and with love in their hearts, and who are driven by equality and fairness, rather than the desire to control and discriminate.

Black women have traditionally been the most intense focus of the white gaze, and online they are amongst the most vulnerable and victimised groups, facing threats both on the grounds of gender and ethnicity. Research by Amnesty International reveals that black women on *Twitter* are 84 per cent more likely than white women to be mentioned in abusive or problematic tweets. The study also revealed that one-in-10 tweets mentioning black women was abusive or problematic, compared to one-in-fifteen for white women. Within online dating specifically, black women are downgraded by male users. A recent blog post by *OkCupid*'s co-founder, Christian Rudder, noted that data collected from heterosexual users showed that the strongest biases were against black women and East Asian men. Most males on the site rated black women as less attractive than women of other ethnicities. It also reported that they receive *25 per cent fewer first messages* on *OkCupid* than women of all other ethnicities.

The statistics on who swipes who overwhelmingly conclude that most white people choose other white people. Research by Gerald Mendelsohn, Professor of Psychology at the University of California, revealed that over 80 per cent of the contacts initiated by white members were to other whites, with only 3 per cent to black members. This tendency is certainly true of the majority of my white friends, who admitted to making selections based on what was most aesthetically familiar. Meanwhile, people of colour receive fewer swipes online, on the grounds of ethnicity. If you are a person of colour who doesn't find whites attractive, there is no problem here, but those who are attracted to people of all ethnicities are at an inherent disadvantage from the outset. As a result, with a vastly narrower field of options, people of colour generally cast a wider net than their white counterparts in their searches. This was certainly true in my case. I don't have a strict type, and the women I have dated over the years have all been very different. Mendelsohn's research found that black daters "were 10 times more likely to contact whites than whites were to contact blacks." Judging by the figures, white male and female daters do not have to worry about being usurped by "sexually hotter" blacks anytime soon. We are at the bottom of the pile.

A more revealing statistic would be to show how popular black people are as targets for hook-ups and one-night-stands, as opposed to relationships, on apps like *Tinder*. The results might show very different numbers. White people appear to have less of a problem with this kind of interaction. Black females, similar to black males, have found themselves on the receiving end of post-colonial sexual stereotypes about possessing a more voracious sexual appetite or outlandish sexual preferences. "There's this assumption that black women – especially if plus-sized – go along the dominatrix line," says Yeboah. Posting on her blog, *Nerd About Town*, she revealed that she often received texts from white male daters that said things like, "you look like a dominant black queen", or "I have such a thing for chocolate". Yeboah, a full-figured black woman, concludes that, "comments such as these are extremely dehumanising to myself and other black women who are only looking for companionship."

While women in general have to be mindful of abusive male behaviour, black women must be additionally mindful of white men with this sexual fetish for their ethnicity. I have cautioned one of my sisters, who is single and online dating, to *beware of white men who just want to fuck you, rather than love you*. One potential sign of this can occur with white men who date black women, but don't see them as potentially being part of their lives. In 2017, Ari Curtis, a 28-year-old New York marketing executive, wrote on her blog, *Least Desirable*, about her experiences dating as an African-American woman. She recalled having drinks in a Brooklyn bar with a white Jewish man. "He was like, 'Oh, yeah, my family would never approve of you,'" she recounted. "Yeah, because I'm black," she replied. True love, as the saying goes, sees no colour, but for some people, it does. Black people online are separated by their ethnicity, and yet our hurtful experiences in love are the same as whites — we have all felt let down, betrayed or heartbroken. But, there are key circumstantial differences. "Black heartbreak" does exist as a distinct condition that describes someone who has been discriminated against in love. For example, a black female online dater might be rejected by black men who prefer white women, or else she may be sought after by white men for sex only, as described.

The disappointments of black women within online dating go some way toward explaining why they are the least prevalent demographic across the apps. After Yeboah's experience, she went through phases of quitting and rejoining, until she finally quit altogether. "I don't see any point," she lamented. It is easy to extrapolate, on the basis of all these findings, how a black woman can end up feeling more angry, more sad, more cynical and more disillusioned than a white person about the online dating experience, as her conditions are that much harsher. This is driving the growth of "splinter apps" which cater to specific niches unsatisfied with mainstream offerings . Dating sites such as *SingleMuslim* (for Muslims) and *JSwipe* (for Jews) have launched, alongside specialist black dating apps such as *BlackCupid*, *Soul Singles* and *BlackPeopleMeet*, which attempt to create a safe space where people of colour can find each other and escape discrimination.

Despite Internet dating's reputation for facilitating interactions with people who would never otherwise have met, it seems that, in America, it may not be breaking down racial barriers, at least not very quickly. At present a few people cross the colour line, but not many. "We are nowhere near the post-racial age," says Mendelsohn. But not everyone agrees. Researchers from the University of Essex and the University of Vienna in Austria, recently published a statistical study of rates of interracial marriages in America, concluding that upward rates have moved in tandem with the growth of online dating. "It is intriguing that shortly after the introduction of the first dating websites in 1995, like *Match*, the percentage of new marriages created by interracial couples increased rapidly," said researchers Josue Ortega and Philipp Hergovich. The increase became steeper in the 2000s, when online dating became more popular, and further in 2014, when the proportion of interracial marriages jumped again. "It is interesting that this increase occurs shortly after the creation of *Tinder*," they speculated. The data doesn't conclude that online dating is the sole cause of the spike in interracial marriages, but they contend that it does appear to correlate with the culture's growth.

My own experience of contacting white daters in the UK correlates with the research findings that black people are low in the rankings. Approximately two out of 10 (or 20 per cent) of the women across *Tinder*, *Bumble*, *Hinge* and *happn*, responded to me contacting them — although I would not conclude that race was necessarily the reason for my 80 per cent rejection rate. It could partly be attributed to the fact that I, like many men, tend to swipe the more attractive-looking women, from whom responses are lower, due to the overwhelming volume of messages they receive. By contrast, in terms of searching out black women, of all the single London females I scrolled through across the four dating apps, easily over a thousand faces, I estimate that only five per cent (50) were black. And this number dwindled even further when I assessed whether or not I liked their personalities or found them attractive. I eventually went on dates with five black women, and even though I connected with them all racially, they didn't work out, and for reasons not connected to race. I was too old for one of them, at 52, as she wanted to have a child with a younger man, while another had only been single for a few weeks and was not over her ex. The other three all had amazing personalities, but I just didn't feel a spark. I wanted to, but I just didn't. Because there are fewer black women online, the consequences of dates with them not working out is bigger, as you just don't know when you might meet another one.

The lowest response rate I got was from South and East Asian women. In fact, I only ever received two responses from these groups, and none resulted in dates. In the UK, these groups are socially more insular, and tend not to mix.

It is a rare sight across the London landscape to see an Asian woman partnered with a black man. In the other direction, the vast majority of women who sought me out were white, which entirely makes sense, as that is the largest ethnic group using the apps. On this basis, it is not much of a stretch to see how, in probability terms, a black man or woman might end up with a white partner here in the UK. There are just more of them. Choice online is governed less by racial preference and more by availability.

Abuses against minorities are spread far wider than just to black people. Amongst men for example, it is not black males, but East Asians who are bottom of online dating's desirability rankings, both within heterosexual and gay relationships — and not only are they on the bottom, they are also often subjected to racial abuse as a result. Racism has long been a problem on gay dating app *Grindr*, for example. A 2015 paper by Australian researchers found that 96 per cent of users had viewed at least one profile that included some sort of racial discrimination, and more than half said they'd been victims of racism. More than one-in-eight admitted including text on their profile indicating that they discriminated on the basis of race. In 2018, NPR reported the case of Jason, a 29-year-old gay Filipino from Los Angeles, who had received messages from daters such as, "I don't date Asians — sorry, not sorry;" and, "You're cute...for an Asian," when he first signed up seven years prior. "It was really disheartening," he recalled. "It really hurt my self-esteem." Some of the comments posted on *@GrindrRacism* are even more shocking, ranging from statements like, "only into white guys", all the way through to, "shouldn't [black people] be in the fields, picking cotton?" Asian women are also targets. One 26-year-old online dater of Mauritian-Asian ancestry confessed to *The Independent* newspaper that she'd also faced discrimination due to her ethnicity. "On *Tinder*, a guy messaged me saying, 'I have never shagged an Asian before, let's meet so I can tick it off'," she said.

No one is surprised by the fact that in a racist society, racist elements surface online — but what is different is the fact that the Internet, as a predominantly written rather than verbal medium, means racist comments are easier to track, measure and share. There is no hearsay about racism written within someone's dating profile. It is there for all to see as an indelible barometer of its enduring presence within society.

As well as bringing people together, social apps have now been weaponised by abusers in ways that do exactly the opposite — and their owners have been slow to tackle issues such as racism and sexism within their networks. This is partly because the founders are mostly white and male, and so questions about how to prevent racial abuse — an issue that does not affect them or their group — were not uppermost in their minds when devising their products. All of them — *Facebook*, *Twitter*, *Tinder*, etc — have been reactive rather than active in taking steps to combat racial and other forms of abuse. The established pattern is, they wait until it happens, wait until people are already hurt, and then hurriedly mobilise, eager to contain any negative PR that may result.

One way in which dating sites have tried to tackle racist abuse is by allowing users to filter matches according to ethnicity. This has proved controversial. Online dating operates on the premise that everything is categorized. Humans are filleted into component parts, which people can then search and filter — height, age, religious persuasion — and yes, race. People do not exist as whole entities, but rather, as a kit of parts, for which ethnicity is the most unsettling option. This explains why so few sites allow users to filter according to ethnicity. But some do. *Match* is an example. While I was on their site I found a number of white and East Asian women whose profiles I liked, but when I clicked on them, they had specified that they didn't want to date black men. Some are offended by this feature, and regard it as racist, but I welcome it. Being filtered out of someone's searches within online dating is not the same for example, as being discriminated against in the job market. While an employer should not have the right to exclude an ethnic minority from the workplace, it is preposterous to suggest that a white person should be made to engage with a black or Asian person when it comes to their choice of who to date or have sex with. For example, I would rather not waste my time sending well-crafted messages to racists, who therefore will not respond, or else may send me a racist comment back. It is much better to focus instead on the ones who do like me. The issue then, is not that one ethnicity likes or dislikes another, it is more the permissive and unregulated use of racist language within the apps messaging systems, perpetrated by abusers toward those they do not find attractive. Dating app developers could resolve this by allowing users to put their racial preferences within their profile settings, like *Match* does, and then to simply allow the algorithm to filter out those they don't want to see, so they do not show up in searches for either party. *Keeping people apart that have no attraction for each other is the critical objective*, thereby reducing the possibility for racist language being scripted.

*

At the end of this extended discovery phase about how blacks are perceived within online dating, I actually began a relationship with the white woman who admitted to swiping me because she thought I was a playa, thinking that she could have fun without commitment. On our first date I was pleased to tell her that she was wrong in her assumption, and that I was online dating because I sought a long-term relationship. This surprised her, smashing her misconception of me as some kind of Nigerian James Bond who would give her a proper seeing to with my super-sized, baby-denting dick, and then abruptly leave. Instead of getting angry, I joked with her about it.

"So I've messed up your plan," I said proudly.

"You have. Damn," she replied. "What kind of brother are you — looking for love and all that?"

It just goes to show — love can sprout from anywhere. Even from racial stereotypes.

Our relationship developed from here, when she witnessed how much more there was to me than just fuck-meat, and I saw how much more there was to her than subscribing to racial stereotypes. She began taking a real interest in race, and what it is to be a black person in today's society, and this drew us together. In our conversations about our respective insecurities I suggested that dating me would be more troublesome than being with a white man, because of my awareness and experience of discrimination and racism, and the emotional scars I still carry from it. Nevertheless, things began to evolve very quickly to a deeper, more emotional level. The relationship lasted six months, and then floundered, and I am happy to say, not for reasons to do with race.

5

The Black Woman's Guide To Online Dating (The 13 Steps)

As stated in the previous chapter, black women are at the bottom of the Internet dating pool, receiving fewer matches and responses than whites, Asians and other ethnic groups. Therefore, if you are a black woman you will have to put more effort into optimising your online dating profile in order to maximise your chances. So, what are the best practices that may help steer you toward better outcomes? Below are my top recommendations — but they are not just relevant for black women, but for women generally, as well as for men who wish to know more about the concerns of females they seek to connect with.

1. Be Resilient

Because conditions online are that much harsher for black women, they are at greater risk of psychological damage than other ethnic groups. Added to this are the broader side-effects of living within a racist and discriminatory society. These disappointing facts are important for you to know and understand, so you can manage your expectations, as it means it may take you longer to find your match than it does for white women, and you may suffer more as a result. Complaining or dwelling upon this is futile, as it changes nothing — instead you must *decide to act*. You cannot control who is present on the apps or what they do, but you can control *your reaction* to them. Your first task is to avoid being angry, bitter or sad, and instead be strong and resistant to erosion. Think of yourself as a beautiful slab of black granite, standing tall and defiant.

2. Be An Emotional Detective

If you are signed up to any of the mainstream UK dating apps, it is likely that most men who contact you will be white. There are far fewer black singles here than in America for example, and so choices are limited. Of the white men who may message you, your mission is to discover which ones want you for sex or potentially for love. Asking them straight out may be too direct, and may not necessarily yield a clear answer, and so you may have to look for clues elsewhere. Carefully scrutinise the photos they choose to post and what they say within their messaging; ask about their relationship history and how long they have been single, and look closely at how they treat you. Try to assess their level of emotional availability. Learn to be a good detective. If you do not, you will fail.

Learn more about being an emotional detective in chapter 8.

3. Choose Your App(s) Carefully

Many choose *Tinder*, as this is the brand leader, although it retains its reputation as the app for those seeking sex, and so it attracts men with this objective. The majority of its massive user base is white and male, and so black women who sign up may attract those who only see their blackness sexually, and in line with the racial stereotypes previously discussed. The sexual overtures of this group will inevitably expose you to insulting or abusive behaviour, which may prematurely erode your tolerance for online dating as a whole, driving you away from the platforms altogether. Therefore my recommendation is that *no black woman who seeks a long-term relationship should use Tinder*.

A better option is to explore the apps that are less overtly sexual, such as *Bumble* or *Hinge*, or else if your preference is for a black partner, *Match* and *EliteSingles* now allow users to filter according to ethnicity, so you only see those options. Specialist black dating apps are also emerging. *BlackPeopleMeet* is the most popular, although it is currently limited to the USA and Canada. Be aware that the niche apps, though highly targeted, have fewer members than the mainstream options, and so your choices will be more limited, which may mean your search takes longer if you use them exclusively. Remember also that no dating apps are completely free of sex pests and abusers, and so you may still encounter some, whichever option you choose, although their numbers may be smaller.

4. Create Winning Images

Because black women receive fewer responses online, you should not make it easier to be dismissed by posting substandard imagery. Create a great set of pictures of yourself — not just selfies, which are now overused. In tests, photos in which people are smiling, with eyes to camera, and also wearing bright colours, work best. If you are dark-skinned ensure your shots have plenty of light. Do not obscure your face by wearing sunglasses, ski goggles or hats. Get a friend to take some pictures of you instead of doing them all yourself. Alternatively, go one better and hire a professional photographer. This shows daters that you are serious, and willing to go the extra mile to present yourself in the best way. Headshot photographers who specialise in actors portraits can be booked for around £200 ($250). You can justify the expense by also giving copies to friends and family. Do not post any sexually revealing photos (unless of course you are looking for sex). This will only encourage men to view you accordingly. In terms of numbers of images, profiles with three photos or more attract the highest number of responses.

Another option to make your profile stand out is to include video. This is a new addition to dating apps, which very few are using. Video receives *twice the level of engagement* as photos, and so this could increase the number of positive swipes you receive. Keep your posts short — 10 seconds or less — and choose a theme which shows you being funny or creative. Lastly, ensure that you are smiling before you hit record, so the first frame of your video captivates the viewer's attention.

5. Write Something

Where the apps permit, *no person of colour should ever sign up to a dating app without including a written profile*. To not do so invites the possibility for white people to judge you solely along racially stereotypical lines, and to make snap judgements about you, not only sexually, but across other important measures such as integrity or honesty. Unfortunately, race is already a factor within perceptions of trustworthiness, so all the more reason to include some text to counter this. **According to *Bumble*, fully completed profiles incorporating words and images receive 27 per cent more attention. Creating a written profile is your way of saying to the world, but more** importantly to yourself, *I am a human being, I AM A PERSON.* If you are not sure what to say, ask a friend to assist. A great line for a black woman to include is, "I seek someone who wants me for who I am, rather than what I am." Finally, do not connect with anyone who has not read your text — this means they are responding only to *what they see of you aesthetically and sexually* as a black woman.

6. Work Your Profile

Don't make the mistake of thinking that once you have created your online dating resume, that this is the end of the story. Your dating profile is a marketing document, and so you should work the material. *Your profile should never be static.* Each week or two, try uploading a new lead photo, and see what effect it has on who approaches you. Try a different hairstyle, an outfit change or a different smile. Look again at your filter selection, or answer a different set question. Run alternate written profiles also.

7. Use The Apps

It sounds obvious, but those who are most active have the best chance of success. Dating apps are driven by algorithms that reward frequent users and downgrade dormant profiles. Moreover, because black women receive fewer approaches than white women, they simply cannot afford to sit back and wait to be contacted. You have to be proactive, and prepared to reach out first to those you like.

8. Make A Phone Call

If you are unsure about meeting a prospective date after messaging, ask to speak to them on the phone first. (Initially, when you make the call, use the feature on your mobile that allows you to withhold your number). This option is less intrusive than a video-call, and is a good way to get a feel for who the person is, and what their motives may be. Keep your general tone light-hearted and humorous, so it doesn't come across like an interview. As well as asking him questions, invite him to ask questions about you too. How interested is he in who you are and what you do? If the man is white, ask him if he has ever had a relationship with a black woman, and how long it lasted. Any man who has issues with your desire to ask questions is simply not the one for you.

When it comes to actually meeting, those who feel more vulnerable may require extra safeguards. Always meet a first date in daylight in a public place, and never at their home. Ensure you tell someone where you are going, who you are meeting, and what time you expect to be back. If you have the man's phone number, give it to them also.

9. No Sex

Do not have sex until you feel comfortable the person likes you, rather than just the sexual you. You want to avoid white men who think like this:

> *I want to fuck a black woman just to see*
> *what it's like, just to tick it off my list.*

Communicate your motives for holding back from sex at the outset, so they are aware why, as a black woman, you need to be specially cautious. The men who like you will understand, and wait, and the ones who just want sex will quickly depart. Be aware that with the best of intentions this may not always work, as online dating is predicated on a fast turnover of results, but it is always better to have a strategy than not.

10. Take Regular Breaks

Online dating can be particularly mentally gruelling for black women, and you may very quickly feel drained and cynical. Counter this by taking regular breaks to rest and be free of constantly checking your mobile. Create your own schedule, whether it means a break every second week, or month. Alternatively, you could restrict your usage to peak periods, which are Sunday's and Monday's, plus daily commuting hours of 9am and 6pm. Most activity drops away after 9pm.

In terms of usage, most apps recommend approximately 30 minutes per day, but many people are active for much longer. A good strategy to avoid overuse is to restrict usage to weekends, and to set up your dating accounts on a spare phone, if you have one, with a different SIM. Leave it at home so you are not tempted to access it during the day, or else give it to a friend to look after until the weekend.

11. Don't Be Alone

A black woman who is working her way through the difficulties of online dating does not have to be isolated in her quest. There are many others out there who are in exactly the same position. Why not start a group and share your experiences and tips with each other? One never knows where this could lead. You could start a movement. #BlackLivesMatter began with a single tweet. Black Girls Who Code grew out of a dearth of ethnic minority women in tech. Apps such as *Bumble* already have features allowing users to connect for business or friendships, as opposed to just dating. You could start there. If you are unhappy with dating apps because the matches do not work, or because you keep being trolled or abused by men, instead of quitting angrily and staying single, why not mobilise your group to lobby the dating platforms to do more? Big corporations tend not to listen to individuals, but they do listen to groups, particularly if not doing so means bad press or revenue loss. The bigger the group, the more power you have.

12. Retain A Sense Of Humour

Black people are fully aware that society discriminates against them in many ways. Using humour as a coping mechanism is a very practical response to the negativities of online dating, and indeed life generally. Think about how important comedy is within the black tradition as an antidote to pain, and how it has spawned a plethora of stand-up comedians, from Richard Pryor to Kevin Hart.

13. Outsource Vetting

If you are fed up with the whole exercise of online dating, or you do not have the emotional armour for it, consider letting your best friend field enquiries for you instead. You never know, they may actually choose more wisely than you do. Using this method shields you from the digital shrapnel that can be such an unpleasant part of the culture. The way it should work is that they vet enquiries on your behalf, then present you with a shortlist of candidates for you to contact. They should never contact people on your behalf.

*

If you find yourself resisting these recommendations, ask yourself why. As a black woman you may feel more negatively about online dating as a result of encountering more extreme experiences. But those who think negatively about life often tend to behave that way too. Could this be further affecting your success online? Ensure not to let negativity sabotage your efforts. You deserve the same success as anybody else, but this belief starts within you.

See chapter 8 for more about creating the best dating profile.

6

Are All Online Daters Rubbish? (Or Are You The Problem?)

There are no decent people online.

This is the phrase I hear most often from critics of online dating, or those who have tried it and then left disappointed and disillusioned. But is it true? Can it really be true when the apps are full of doctors, scientists, nurses, cleaners, yoga teachers, human rights lawyers, journalists, artists and so on — in other words, exactly the same people as those walking around offline? The truth is embarrassingly obvious, and yet people often refer to online daters as if we belong to a separate sub-human species of three-headed trolls.

Consider this instead — could it be that it is not online daters who are the problem — but you.

Many angry Internet daters or disillusioned ex-daters who deride the practice are themselves less than fit for purpose, having posted online profiles that are sub-optimal. Anyone who has uploaded poor quality photography, not written any copy, or else has not recovered emotionally from their previous relationship before going online in the first place, is adding to the problems within online dating culture, rather than adopting a workable strategy for finding a partner. Nevertheless, I regularly hear daters in this category referring to how many arseholes there are within online dating — and of course there are — *but what if you are the arsehole?*

Consider this example: let's say you matched with someone on a dating app, and then after exchanging a few messages, they ghosted you. You might conclude, "That person ghosted me, what a fucking arsehole." But what if the reason they ghosted you is because, without realising it, you wrote something inappropriate that put them off? It might be, in fact, that you are the arsehole. After all, how would you know? Most of us surround ourselves with friends who endorse rather than criticise who we are. You may consider yourself a catch, and your friends may tell you that you are great, but they do not know what you are really like in the depths of a relationship, especially when things go wrong. What if you are actually a nightmare? Many of us skip this kind of self-analysis when assessing whether or not to begin online dating, or even if we are fit for purpose. "A big part of finding the right partner, is being the right partner," says Samantha Joel, Psychologist at the University of Utah.

Sometimes I wonder how many times I have been the arsehole on my Internet dates, especially early on after my break-up, when my emotional damage was at maximum. On several occasions I have changed my mind about women I matched with, after exchanging texts with them and getting a feel for who they were. In three cases I remember, I decided the women were narcissists and so I ended the chat. This always seems abrupt, although the alternative — to lecture them on what is, in fact, only my opinion about who they are — would be inappropriate. The women in question might describe me as the arsehole, because I swiped right on them, and then after some chat, ghosted them.

We all like to think that everybody else is the arsehole,

and that we are the lovely ones, the blameless ones. We are often reluctant to consider our own culpability within events, because it means potentially criticising one's own personality, and possibly concluding that we may not be the amazing people we think we are — that in fact, we might have issues and insecurities that are contributing to our failures. One of the reasons some of us are so deeply affected by the routine rejection and abandonment of online dating is because they activate insecurities we already have from our past. A person who has abandonment issues from their childhood for example, may be sent reeling from dating apps after being perpetually ghosted by its users. Their response may be to conclude that there are "no decent people" on there, when in reality they are simply reacting to being triggered. Old wounds open fresh, and fractures appear that are more magnified and therefore more terrifying than before.

I have a mantra that, before blaming the other party for what goes wrong in online dating's interactions, it is always good practice to first ask yourself:

> *How did I contribute to the event, and*
> *what could I have done differently?*

All dating apps would be radically different environments if all its participants accepted some responsibility for what it has become, because after all, we, the people who sign up for it, are ultimately collectively responsible for how good or bad its interactions are. And in accepting this, you acknowledge that behaviourally, you may not be as lovely as you think. In fact, we may all, without realising it, have a little bit of Darth Vader in us, in terms of our conduct online, and in real life.

This "badness" often surfaces in reaction to the realisation of how unspecial we all are as online daters. Of course, you are special, we all are — you are special to your friends, your parents, your children, work colleagues and so on; you are kind, compassionate, smart and loving, you give to charity, you are kind to animals, you recycle your waste, help old ladies across the road and volunteer at the local food bank — but online you are simply one of thousands. You are just a face, a trading card, a number in the scroll, an item in a vending machine. In the offline world of traditional values, the word "special" means, *to be distinct from others* — but online, where you only exist as part of a large carousel, you are indistinct. You think you're hot? There's hotter. You think you're smart? There's smarter. You think you're funny? There's funnier. How can any of us think of ourselves as a catch within an arena in which everyone is a catch, and so therefore no one is. In the swipe-fest that is dating apps, no one really matters to anyone because there is always another someone *less than a second away*.

Accepting this truth is key to getting the most out of Internet dating. The first thing that must go is your ego. Ego does not work online — only humility does. You must relinquish the idea that you are better than anybody else in the queue, and that therefore you deserve more, and instead accept being swiped away — *just as you yourself swipe others away*. Ghosting presents a good example of the problem of ego. The reason being ghosted hurts is because your ego gets burned — someone out there doesn't like you, doesn't think you are amazing, or perhaps does not recognise your amazingness. This disrupts your view of yourself. But, the lower your ego, the less you will be hurt. In our social media-driven world in which people are obsessed with self-image, accepting ones own absolute unspecialness — in effect becoming the *anti-narcissist*, who does not think constantly of how great they think they are — may be the healthiest position to take.

Alternatively, if you are not the arsehole, maybe it is the apps that are the problem. One of the factors that make them difficult to navigate is that most of us believe all online daters are looking either for sex or a relationship, whereas in reality there are *five different levels of user,* each of whom have different objectives. They are:

1. Those who look, swipe right, match, text and meet (for a relationship).
2. Those who look, swipe right, match, text and meet (for sex).
3. Those who look, swipe right, match and text only.
4. Those who look, swipe right and match only.
5. Those who look and swipe left only.

Each of these levels represent different degrees of fear within the psyche of online daters, with level 5 being the most fearful group, and level 1 the least. The difficulty is that all five levels are present within dating apps simultaneously, existing within one massive, unsorted cocktail in which each category is totally unidentifiable from another. When an online dater first interacts with someone, they have no idea whether they are connecting with a level 1, 2, 3, 4 or 5, despite what the person might say. What is clear though, is that a match can only happen with someone who is in the same category as you. A level 4 doesn't work with a level 1, and a level 2 doesn't work with a level 3, and so on. If the dating apps could separate each of the five levels into their respective groupings, everyone would have what they wanted. Instead, what we have is, by definition, utter chaos.

The least proactive users are level 5. They are voyeurs who are there only to look, and no more, which is why they swipe left. They might be people who have recently broken up with their partners and are therefore not yet ready to engage, but are curious to see who is out there. Alternatively they could be groups of friends on a night out, or people at home who are using the apps game-like interface as an entertainment device to keep themselves amused by mocking the ugly and admiring the pretty. This is the cruellest sub-group. For them, the presence of lonely singles searching for love online is Saturday night comedy. The dating apps compete for their attention with other social platforms, and with entertainment mediums such as *iTunes* and *Netflix*. Level 5s will often "double-screen" — use different entertainment platforms simultaneously, such as watching television while scrolling through the dating apps.

Level 4s seek to look, swipe right and match only. They go one step further than level 5s in actually connecting with people on apps like *Tinder*. They swipe right on those they find attractive, but no more than that. In this guise *Tinder* is *Instagram* for those who like looking at faces. It is a social media app rather than a device for dating. Other level 4s typically seek to match as a way of *collecting endorsements* in order to re-boot their self-esteem, feed their narcissism or even to boost their *Instagram* followers by directing people to their account. A 2017 survey compiled by loan finance firm, LendEDU asked 9,761 millennials about dating on *Tinder*. Forty-five per cent confessed that they use it only for "confidence-boosting procrastination". Relationship psychologist Madeleine Mason Roantree explains how this works. "When we match it's almost like a little dopamine hit," she explains. "It lights up the pleasure sensor in our brain, so it can be quite addictive." This rush of pleasure works better for women than men, particularly on apps like *Tinder*, because "likes" happen faster and in greater numbers. Research conducted in 2016 by Queen Mary University, London, found that "Male profiles slowly build up matches over time, with a very shallow gradient of increase. In contrast, female profiles gain rapid popularity, achieving in excess of 200 matches in the first hour."

The behaviour of level 4s is revealed by the volume of messages sent between online daters that go unanswered. Sociologists from the University of Michigan study into online dating, published in 2018, reported that only 23 per cent received responses. Level 4s would feature heavily amongst the remaining 77 per cent — that is, people receiving messages from those they have matched with, who have no intention of communicating back. Dating apps are often criticised for the way they reduce humans to a flicker-book of options, like a fast food menu — but the difference here is that this a menu that you mostly can't "eat", because the majority of people you contact will ignore you.

While researching this book I interviewed someone who is at level 4 — an attractive Swedish woman in her early twenties, working in London. On the day we met she had downloaded *Hinge*, and hurriedly compiled a sub-standard profile consisting of two and three-word answers to questions, plus some poor quality imagery. Nevertheless, she had attracted 50 responses from men who wanted to match with her, within just a few hours.

"Are you not interested in any of them?" I asked.

"No. It's jokes really."

"What do you mean?"

"Just having fun. I'm not really interested."

"So then, what are you getting out of it?"

"I just go on there when I'm feeling a bit low or whatever, and then when I see that guys like me, that's all I need, and so I just delete."

By contrast, a level 3 — who looks, swipes right, matches, texts, but never meets — may only be looking for a pen-pal in order to feel wanted, or to counter feelings of loneliness, or else they may simply enjoy flirting. They could also be people who are already in relationships, and therefore have no real intention of meeting. A 2015 study of 47,000 global Internet users by consumer research firm GlobalWebIndex, claimed that 42 per cent of *Tinder*'s user base were either married or were already in relationships — a claim the dating app vehemently denied.

Online dating profiles are riddled with level 1 daters (those seeking to meet for relationships), complaining about level 3s who never want to meet; "I'm not into endless messaging, so if you're looking for a pen-pal, please swipe left," is a common refrain. On many occasions I have been involved in exchanges with people in this category, without realising it. The preliminary chat goes fantastically well, and then as soon as I broach the subject of meeting up, they ghost me. Its as if a bomb has gone off within them:

Shit, he wants to meet up. I better run.

There are many similar stories from frustrated daters. When 30-year-old Londoner Sara Scarlett moved to Dubai in 2015, she signed up to *Tinder*, but found converting swipes to dates difficult. "You spend ages chatting to these guys and then they don't even want to go for a coffee," she told a BBC reporter in February 2018. "There are hundreds of time-wasters, losers, and just general Muppets on there who have nothing better to do than mess you around."

The journey from online search to real life is just a step too far for level 3s. They can't go through with it. But go through with what? Coffee? This is how fearful, how entrenched within our caves we've become, when a person can't face someone new over a cappuccino. We only feel safe in our disconnected digital state, behind our smartphones looking at pictures.

Levels 1 and 2 — those who actually want to meet up — are the only sets who correspond to the current definition of what Internet dating is. The intention of level 2s is to meet for sex. These members can become very frustrated, as there is no way to clearly identify which online daters have the same intention as they do. As a result they adopt a scattergun approach — which is to ask everybody. This explains why "No ONS, no hook-ups" is the most used phrase within the dating bios of older female daters. It is a direct response to level 2s bombarding them with requests for sex. According to the Queen Mary University study, 49 per cent of male respondents stated that they use *Tinder* for one-night-stands, compared to just 15 per cent of women.

Level 1s are those seeking love and a relationship. Ironically, they share the same objective as level 2s — which is to meet people — but their intentions are the polar opposite. Level 1s are also a very frustrated group, as they are perpetually exerting energy into trying to meet people who don't want to be met. Without realising it, they are interacting with those from all the other levels who are clogging up the network with their various intentions, none of which is to actually date. Their frustrations are understandable when one considers how many of these non-daters there are online. Research by America's Pew Research Centre reveals that a third of US online daters have never actually been on a date — and this figure is even higher with younger digital daters. Another survey by LendEDU polled 3,852 US college students who had online dated, revealing that 71 per cent had never been on a date. Figures from research conducted by Queen Mary University are higher still. According to their study 10 per cent or fewer of matches on *Tinder* resulted in an actual meet-up. When the numbers are this high, the primary objective that the apps had at start-up — to help people meet — becomes critically eroded. Sociologist Michael Rosenfeld, who has studied the field, seems to agree: "Given how few actual face-to-face dates seem to be obtained through *Tinder* and the phone dating apps, it is possible that the main utility of phone dating apps for heterosexuals is for flirting or for browsing pictures, rather than for dating or for hooking up," he says.

This is all bad news if you are looking for love on the Internet. Put more simply, if all five levels were equally represented online in terms of numbers, each person in each group would have a 1-in-5 chance (20 per cent) of connecting with someone with the same intention. However, in practice, the size of each group is not equal, which means that those who seek to actually meet someone for love, or even a hook-up, may have a significantly *less than 20 per cent chance* of success. With odds like these, it comes as no surprise then, that for many people, online dating does not work, and that "there are no decent people on there".

To add even more complexity to it all, the intentions of

those within the five categories are also shifting and becoming more diverse. Many university students for example, instead of dating, use apps like *Hinge* as a form of *LinkedIn*-lite, for professional hook-ups, because they find it less formal and easier to target those within their age range. The other element that is constantly shifting are the numbers who populate the five categories. *All levels are fluid rather than static* positions, with people constantly teleporting between categories with changes in their emotional states. How long does it take for a level 5 to shift to a level 1, or vice-versa, for example? The answer is — it could take a microsecond, or a lifetime.

*

Throughout history humans have always appropriated new technology, inventing new and often surprising uses that their inventors did not envisage — and not all of them have been of benefit. The inventors of household glue for example, did not imagine that users would one day start inhaling it instead of using it to bond items together. The same is true of dating apps and how people use them today. A tool invented to help people meet for love or sex, is now used as an entertainment device to mock other humans, or else as a means to counter loneliness, or to boost one's sense of wellbeing. The mixed intentions of its users have made the apps more complicated to navigate and harder for each category to find what they are looking for.

As a level 1, I came across this problem some time ago when I was stood up on a first date by someone who, unknown to me, was a level 3. There is nothing that challenges your view of yourself and dents your ego more than this. It is one of the lowest moments in Internet dating — sitting in a bar alone, and slowly realising with the passing of time that my proposed date was not coming, and was actually somewhere else, perhaps laughing at me, having abandoned me to my own silent humiliation. Up to that point I may have seen myself as a wonderful person, attractive, witty, totally lovely, yes, totally, totally lovely, no doubt — but the person who stood me up obviously did not agree. I thought she was the arsehole for not turning up, and for not telling me, but maybe she didn't turn up because she thought I was the arsehole. Or maybe she would never have turned up in the first place because level 3s don't meet? Who knows?

7

The Emotional Detective (New Columbo)

The American television show, *Columbo*, starring the late Peter Falk, is the greatest detective series of all time. It circumvents the key premise of the murder-mystery detective genre, by telling the viewer who the killer is right at the beginning of each programme. Lieutenant Columbo then proceeds to uncover the evidence to prove the case. When it comes to online dating, we should all aim to be as good as Lieutenant Columbo at interpreting clues. We need to become *emotional detectives* — analysing the words and imagery daters post about themselves to make informed conclusions about personality types, and therefore their suitability as potential partners. Right now many of us miss or ignore vital indicators when assessing candidates, and end up choosing those who are not right for us. This is because we tend to focus on the aesthetic, sexual, professional and social reasons we are drawn to people. "Research shows when people are evaluating photos of others, they are trying to access compatibility on not just a physical level, but a social level," said Dr. Jessica Carbino, ex-in-house sociologist at *Tinder* and *Bumble*. "They are trying to understand, 'Do I have things in common with this person?'" But the key thing that is missing here, and that is harder to assess, is *psychological compatibility*. This information can only be obtained by being like Columbo.

There are three basic rules to being an emotional detective:

1. As online, so offline

In other words, *everything a person does online denotes character offline*. If someone mocks you, or puts you down during your online exchanges, this person is likely to do the same thing in real life; if a person appears to be hiding in the photos they post, they probably are; if a person posts multiple images of themselves with material things, they might be struggling to express themselves emotionally; if someone seems keen to answer your questions, but does not ask you anything in return, they may be a narcissist.

2. Photography is truth

Much of the imagery posted within dating profiles is designed to conceal rather than reveal. Many hide behind hats and sunglasses. I have seen profiles in which daters are wearing dark glasses in *every single photo*. People often maintain that they enjoy wearing shades because they think they look cool, or that they somehow make them "look better". But dark glasses work by *removing the eyes* from view, making us appear less human. How is this "cool?" How is hiding ones eyes a better look than revealing them?

Others choose to post images in which they are too far away to be seen, or else they are looking away from camera, sometimes down at the ground, as if they are somehow ashamed, embarrassed or afraid. Many pictures show the back of people's heads, or else with their faces obscured by long hair, or shrouded in silhouette. On one occasion I was contacted by a woman who's lead image consisted of a shot of her from behind on a bicycle, riding away. What was she trying to tell me? Was she shy? Did she have trust issues? Was she cycling away from intimacy, away from being known? More disturbingly, others offer sexualised images featuring their naked or semi-naked torsos with their own heads digitally severed. Why do daters choose to represent themselves in these ways? If you are open, happy and keen to be known, why would you choose images that conceal? We are all the editors-in-chief of our own narratives, and so these choices are not accidents, but hint at unspoken, unresolved issues. So, what is going on?

There are three reasons online daters obscure their faces:

Shy.
Insecure about their looks.
Hiding something.

It is difficult at first glance to know which of the three are in play when viewing someone's profile photos. They could be signalling that they are not really single, or that they are, but are emotionally unavailable, or that they are fearful about dating, or else that they are hiding something else.

Early on in my online dating experience I went on a date with a woman who'd concealed her face in her profile photos, and as it turned out, she was concealing something in real life too. As we sat down and got talking, she announced that in fact she was not quite single. Our conversation played out like this:

"So, you're still with your partner then?" I said disappointedly. "And child?"

"Yes."

"And you all still live together?"

"Yes."

"So…er, what are you doing, online dating?"

"Well, things have been bad for a bit, so I just thought…."

"But, you're not single."

"I know. But I will be — soon. When I sort things out. Maybe in three months or so, maybe we can meet up again."

"Really? You think?"

On the other hand, amongst the concealers there are those who legitimately choose not to be identified online for professional or social reasons, such as therapists, teachers, celebrities, those who work in the security services, people with facial disfigurements and so on. In these cases some resort to wearing disguises, or else posting place-holder images of sunsets, landscapes, cuddly toys or animals instead. I once came across a profile in which someone had posted a picture of a llama instead of their face. Or perhaps it was posted by a llama. An online llama. A llama with an iPhone.

ACTION:

When assessing the imagery within online dating profiles, consider whether the person is trying to be open or not. Being photographically transparent in the majority of imagery implies honesty, openness and emotional readiness, while concealing suggests hesitancy, fear or that they may be hiding something. For some, there may be a legitimate reason why they can't reveal their identity online. Nevertheless, consider whether or not in your choice of partner, you are looking for a revealer or a concealer. If you choose the latter, you may want to ask yourself this:

> *Why am I drawn to someone who is hiding something? What is it in me that wants this?*

Liars are easier to spot if you closely analyse their text. According to a 2011 study by Catalina Toma, Assistant Professor of Communication Arts at the University of Wisconsin-Madison, liars tend to use fewer first-person pronouns. According to Toma, this is a method of creating a psychological distance between the liar and the person they are messaging. Liars use more negative words, such as "not" and "never" — which is another way of creating a barrier. They also use fewer emotional adjectives such as "sad" or "upset," and they write shorter online profiles, as it is easier not to get caught if they say less.

The best performing profile photos are the ones in which the subject is smiling, and with their eyes to camera. I have seen some amazing examples in which women are doing this in every photo, although I find this to be rare. What I see more often is sadness — a collective sadness spread like a contagion throughout the app's card deck scroll. One can only wonder about the causes, the individual stories of pain, disappointment, betrayal or trauma. Whatever their personal narratives, what is clear is how *unrepaired* they are. How unrepaired we all are. Those who post pictures of themselves looking glum or even angry send the opposite message to those who smile. It is very telling that of all the imagery a person has of themselves, they choose the ones in which *they appear to be troubled*. As curators of their own profiles, they are sub-consciously telling us something here, and that is — *if I look sad in my photos, then I am sad.* Given the choice, I would rather not date someone who is miserable, or who spends their time looking miserable, or who posts pictures of themselves looking miserable. But this can get difficult when there are more online daters looking sad than there are looking happy. There are many startling examples, and some amusing ones too. Several times I have come across profiles in which daters have uploaded image after image of themselves looking distinctly glum, with a written accompaniment stating that, "I'm actually more smiley in real life." *So why not post those pictures then? Gee!*

I have also been guilty of "glum face". This is the opening portrait I used on my dating profile. While my eyes are facing camera, which is good, I am not smiling, suggesting I was less than happy when I chose it, very soon after my break-up.

ACTION:
Closely examine the photos of those you are connecting with, and the expressions on their faces. How many images feature them smiling? How many images feature them half-smiling, as if they are putting on a brave face? How many feature them looking totally sad? If you are drawn to the face of someone who looks unhappy, ask yourself why. If you are a sad person who is attracted to sadness in others, this could be a match, but if you seek someone happy, be sure to select someone who looks happy in at least some of their profile images. It sounds simple enough, but it is amazing how many of us do not do this.

There is a body of research that suggests that the type of face a person has influences engagement levels. The reason that online dating protocols advise against wearing anything that obscures the face is because people use this to make fast judgments about personality and attractiveness, and therefore to determine whether or not someone would make a worthy mate. Psychologists refer to this as *thin slicing*. In a survey conducted by *Tinder*, a group of females were shown pictures of male models, and were asked to swipe left or right according to their attraction to them. In almost every instance, they swiped left on those men with chiselled faces. When asked why, they said they looked unkind, or too full of themselves. "Men with softer jaw lines indicate that they have more compassion," says Carbino. Other research also supports the idea that character traits may be read through physiognomy. A 2009 study by the Department of Psychology at the Martin-Luther University in Halle, Germany claimed to be able to determine how extrovert a person is by looking at a single photo, while a 2016 study from researchers at Columbia Business School claimed to be able to predict whether or not the person was trustworthy by examining the details of their face.

ACTION
Drawing conclusions about a person's character solely from their facial features may not provide you with an accurate picture. Confirm or deny your assumptions by reading their profile copy to get a fuller picture. If they have not written anything about themselves, it may be better to move on.

Perhaps the most inappropriate photography present within online dating profiles are the images of single parents with their young children. In terms of protocol, this is as bad as it gets. The children's right to privacy is breached here. Invariably they have not been consulted about whether or not they are comfortable about their faces being featured on a public app for anybody in the country to look at. According to America's Statistic Brain Research Institute, up to 10 per cent of sex offenders use online dating to connect with new people. Of course, parents intend no harm in posting these images, but in their eagerness to illustrate that their kids are part of the package that a prospective suitor must buy into, their children are thrust forward in the photography. Online daters are simply unaware this is bad practice, and a turn-off for many, as nobody tells them, and the apps do not include that information. But shouldn't they know better? Think about it like this: if you went on a first date with someone you met online, would you bring your children along and introduce them to a total stranger? Probably not — so why do it online?

ACTION:

Think about whether or not you want to date someone who has not thought about protecting their children from the digital gaze of strangers. At the very least it suggests carelessness. It may not in practice be a deal-breaker for a potential relationship, but rather a point for discussion between you. If you are a parent posting these images, consider that the best way to inform daters that you have children is simply to say so within your written profile. If somebody writes, "mother to two gorgeous boys", the reader understands what that means without having to actually see their faces. This reinforces the importance of having a written accompaniment to your profile, instead of just images.

There is a disconnect between many of the images posted by certain middle-aged male online daters and the target audience of women within their age range. These men are fond of images of themselves posing with sedated tigers while on some exotic holiday, or brandishing large fish they have caught, or posturing in bare-chested mirror selfies in the gym or bathroom, or parading in their luxury cars, motorbikes and yachts, or posing outside their lavish homes. Meanwhile, many female online daters are laughing at the images that these men think will impress them. The themes promoted within them — hero, warrior, adventurer, rich man, strong man — are out of step with the needs of successful, independent women who have their own cars, houses, and their own fish — and who instead seek love, companionship, kindness, emotional awareness and sensitivity. The cartoonish machismo and materialism offered up by these men acts as a screen to hide the fact that they are lacking in these elements.

ACTION
Be aware of what may be missing from male dater's profiles that focus on sex or materialism as their key offering. Someone who is rich in possessions may be poor emotionally.

Amongst mature daters there is much within their imagery that is distinctly immature in nature. It has become a trend for certain singletons to post images of themselves with their tongues sticking out. Why does the viewer deserve this greeting? Humans first learn to stick their tongues out as children, usually to people they don't like, or who are annoying them, and so the gesture comes across as rude and contemptuous. Similarly, pouting can seem disingenuous, while middle-agers enhancing their portraits with *Snapchat* filters can look childish to anyone out of their teens. The practice also obscures what the person actually looks like, which can be annoying for daters seeking this basic information. Other misleading imagery is also rife, such as singletons who pose with babies and then write, "Don't worry, it's not my baby". *Well, why not just not show that image then? Hello?* There are other classics too, such as those posing in photographs with someone who could be mistaken for their ex-partner. *Why not just not show that picture? Gee!* Then there are those images that show people brandishing large drinks in their hands. What message are they trying to convey here? I am an alcoholic? I need booze as a crutch? I am skilled at holding a glass between my fingers?

ACTION
By analysing the cultural behaviour that people display within their photographs, you can assess whether or not they might be a match. Be aware of immature, careless or even contemptuous signatures within the visual narratives, as these are likely to manifest in real life too.

Mirror selfies have now become overused and outdated as a visual means of communicating within online dating. It has become a recurring cliché to see profiles consisting entirely of photos of a person's own contrived self-image — complete with their phone in shot to complete the cliché. The worst offenders are the narcissistic, sexualised mirror selfies in which men parade their bare torsos in the gym, or women show off in tight, flesh-revealing outfits. Taken together with the absence of text in so many profiles, the primary means of expression (and assessment by the viewer) is aesthetic and sexual, and so in order to compete, this has now been amped up by daters almost to the point of farce. This kind of explicit behaviour we tend to associate with millennials, whose inexperience and naivety we presume leads them to this kind of self-exposure — but more alarmingly it is also present amongst older daters too, who are full of life experience. It is startling to see how ready single, divorced people with children, mortgages, jobs and other big responsibilities are to objectify themselves, especially on *Tinder*, where they freely offer themselves in semi-naked poses, or more disturbing renditions in which they have severed their own heads, focusing solely on their sexual parts, as if they are cuts of beef instead of human beings. People often refer to this carousel of digitised flesh as a meat market, but this is inaccurate, because the carcasses in a meat market are there by force, whereas the flesh on show here is all from volunteers. *These people want to be meat*. This is where *Tinder* crosses paths with reality TV, where people also volunteer to be semi-clad commodities on display for all. For women online, it is one thing for them to have been historically objectified within patriarchal society, but another to self-objectify. On one level, the woman's prerogative to objectify the self may be viewed as a feminist power play, an autonomous move free of male power. Except, the gaze is still male, as it has always been, and the purpose still to titillate men, who provide a very willing audience.

Females who post sexualised or semi-nude images are also more likely to attract sexual comments from men. I once saw a *Tinder* profile of a woman who featured an image of her almost naked torso, with a note that she didn't want to hear from any male creeps who just wanted sex. Of course, sexually abusive male behaviour is unacceptable and cannot be condoned online or anywhere else, but the imagery a woman chooses to publish can do much to encourage or deter this kind of response. But the sexualised imagery that many men post online are often more shocking — dick pics being the most extreme. These images are saying, "I want to have sex with you", or "I want to shock you", or "I want you to notice me", but they are also saying, "I am struggling to communicate with words". When a man sends an image of his penis to a female stranger, he is literally saying:

I am a cock.

In other words, not a man, not a *hu-man* — but an appendage. The irony here is that, in their inarticulacy, dick pics are pinged to people whose dating profiles are often just as inarticulate, featuring a single portrait of the person, with no words. And here we circle right back to the problem of our age — our collective inability to communicate in an era in which everybody thinks they are communicating.

ACTION 1
What can be deduced about online daters whose pictures consist mostly or wholly of selfies? This style of photography has become a mark of convenience, narcissism and also laziness for those who cannot be bothered to create images of a higher compositional quality, and that will make their profile stand out, thereby enhancing their chances of success. If people can't be bothered to present themselves in the best way they can, what else might they not be bothered to do within the potential relationship? Would you be happy dating someone who can't be bothered, as opposed to someone who can?

ACTION 2

Whenever anyone connects with you online using purely sexualised imagery, it is likely that they are struggling to communicate verbally and emotionally. Equally, they may be seeking self-validation to counter feelings of insecurity, self-doubt or unresolved hurt. Is this why some daters publish images of their genitals, or their bare torsos with their own heads severed? If you are looking for sex online, none of this matters, but if you are looking for a long-term relationship, a person's ability to communicate without using sex is critical.

ACTION 3

Some men send unsolicited pictures of genitalia to women via the AirDrop facility on their Apple devices. This feature allows them to anonymously share files with any other Apple devices within the immediate vicinity that has AirDrop turned on. To prevent this, turn AirDrop off on your iPhone. Go to, Settings > General > AirDrop — switch the setting to "Receiving Off".

One of the things people tend not to disclose within their profiles is the amount of time they have been single. This might make a useful addition to the compulsory information required within the sign-up procedure of future apps. It would give online daters the chance to assess *mate preparedness*. Of course, people could lie, but if someone wrote that they had been single for only one week, it might suggest that the timing was right only for talking or a fling, rather than for a new long-term relationship. On the other hand, if a person had been single for many years this could suggest a different issue. During my time online dating I was surprised by the number of women who had not been in relationships for *five and sometimes 10 years*. Some had become *boyfriend-proof*. This happens when their sense of being alone crystallises to the point where they can no longer adjust to having a partner, and the "disruption" it might cause to the single life they have carefully constructed. Some have lived alone for so long that they can no longer envisage sharing a space with a partner. For those affected, the prospect of having a boyfriend has become the alien culture, while being alone has become the norm. And yet at the same time, they still feel a boyfriend-shaped hole within them, which is why they are online dating.

ACTION

Before you embark upon a first date, politely ask how long the person has been single. It is difficult to draw any firm conclusions from their answer, whether it has been for a short or a long period, because no one can put a timeframe on a person's readiness, recovery, or availability, but nevertheless it will give you the chance to consider whether or not it may be important to any proposed partnership. For some the condition may simply be circumstantial. Someone may have been single for one week, but the relationship could have "died" years earlier. To take another example, a single mum with very young children who lives in a remote town could find herself single for years because there are no available men locally, or else the ones who are there are put off by the fact that she has young kids. Meanwhile for others, the reasons for their long-term single status may be of a more emotional nature. Many put the reason down to "just not meeting the right one", but the lengths of time involved suggest that there may also be other issues at play that remain unresolved, and that are not acknowledged within the self-assessment narrative.

I once read the profile of a woman on *Guardian Soulmates* that was entitled, "Heartbroken". The word she'd chosen to introduce herself to the online dating community promoted the fact that she was hurting from her recent break-up and was therefore emotionally unavailable — but simultaneously, here she was online, looking for someone to soothe her discomfort. On another occasion I was contacted by a woman who was dealing with the terrible circumstances of two family members who were both dying of different illnesses at the same time. What she needed was emotional support, but because she didn't have a partner, she was on *Tinder*, trying to connect with someone. She was advertising for a boyfriend, and yet she was not in the right frame of mind to start a new relationship. I refer to this contradictory position, this dual intention, as the yes/no. It describes those who occupy the furrow between these two poles, unable to completely shift either way. The central narrative of the yes/no is this:

I want a partner, but I don't.

Yes/no's come in many forms. For example, a serial commitment-phobe who behaves as if they want a relationship is a common variant. This perpetual emotional seesaw between the damaged state and the healed state has become an epidemic within Internet dating, and therefore within society. Online dating has become an auxiliary method by which hurt singletons revalidate themselves and repair their self-esteem. The apps have become like digital intensive care wards that the emotionally wounded check-in to in order get over their ex-partners, as opposed to finding new ones. Ideally, those healing from a break-up would recover offline and then engage after their emotional wounds had healed, but who wants to do that these days, in our busy, time-poor lives, and especially if going online might actually accelerate the healing process? This partly explains why there is such a high volume of daters across the apps who do not actually go on dates. For them, recovery, not dating, is the objective — and right now, the apps seem to work better for this than they do for finding love.

In the period after my break-up I was a classic yes/no. When I first signed up for online dating I convinced myself that I was ready for a new relationship after just a few weeks of being single, while in reality I was still raw with hurt. Of the dates that I actually chose to go on, I was relieved when they didn't work out, when I was able to find fault in the women, because it meant that I could avoid having to navigate the possibility of a relationship when I was clearly not ready. Whenever I considered whether or not I wanted a relationship, my thought process was:

> *Yes, no, no, no, yes, yes, no, yes, no, no, no, yes,*
> *no, yes, yes, yes, absolutely yes, but no, yes, no.*

Now that Internet dating has become part of the healing process, rather than what comes after healing, I later came to realise that the women who I messaged or dated during my time online dating were actually, unwittingly, players in my personal, selfish recovery process. They might not to be happy to learn this news now, because a proportion of them were probably looking for someone who was ready for a committed relationship, as opposed to helping nurse a wounded man through his recovery. They became collateral damage, and without knowing it, everybody is subject to this same role within the cyclical theatre that is modern dating.

One of most fascinating ways that yes/no's manifest is in their profile photographs. Chief amongst them are those images in which an ex-partner has been cropped out of a person's photo, but a slice of their face, body or very often their dismembered hand remains in shot, eerily wrapped around the person's shoulder or waist. It is very telling that people choose to share images like this, now that photography is free, via our smartphones, and anybody can select any picture they like to create their story. The truth is, if you make the decision to feature the dismembered hand of your former partner in any of your profile photos, *it is there because you want it to be there.* The image says:

I am not over my ex. He (or she) still has a hold on me, see?

The past is gone, and yet it remains — the ghostly embrace of the dismembered hand, severed and therefore dead, actually still lives, like the antagonist in a B-movie horror classic. There are also other types of revealing images that yes/no's post, including blurry photos of their faces, or ones in which they are too dark to be seen. In an age of pin-sharp, high-definition photography available to all, why would you choose **images like this? As the editor of your own** news story, *this is your design.* **These "errors" are so obvious that they may be read as unconscious attempts at self-sabotage. In classic** yes/no style those who post images like this seem to be trying *not to attract a partner*, while advertising for exactly the opposite. The photos are designed to fail. In such situations, a psychological gap opens between the person's *conscious intention* — to meet someone great and live happily ever after;

and their *subconscious action* — to not meet that person.

Is it possible that yes/no's who avoid relationships for fear of being hurt are in fact anticipating a possible future, or one that they create in advance, in the present? There is some fascinating scientific research that suggests that this could be true. In 1997 physicists Edwin May and James Spottiswoode conducted a strictly controlled scientific experiment to investigate whether or not humans possess a natural capacity for what is called a *pre-stimulus response* — that is, the ability to react in anticipation of events that have yet to happen. In their study 125 participants aged from 20 to 74 had electrodes placed upon their skin, which were then attached to a machine that measured skin conductance. They were then fitted with noise-cancelling headphones through which they were played either a loud blast of white noise that lasted for one second, or else just silence. The choice between the two options, and also the intervals between activations, were randomly generated, with each participant subjected to 20 consecutive activations. The results defied logic — the researchers recorded a galvanic skin response in the participants, *three seconds in advance* of them actually hearing the sound. *Their nervous systems, channelling their immediate future, appeared to know when the white noise was coming.*

Since May and Spottiswoode's experiment other researchers have replicated these results using mild electric shocks instead of sound. The participants are not *predicting* the future — as the term pre-cognition suggests — but rather, they are *observing* the future, and then transferring the information backwards in time. These sensational discoveries have largely been ignored by the wider scientific community, as they go against our current understanding of reality and biology. But this ability does make evolutionary sense if viewed as part of the natural human survival instinct. The ability to sense danger in the immediate future would have been a useful line of defence against predators amongst early *Homo sapiens* 200,000 years ago. It may just be that most of us have lost touch with what is actually a natural skill we all possess.

Is it possible then, that commitment-phobic daters could be channelling the possibility of future hurt at the hands of partners they have yet to even meet? Could the reason you are relationship averse right now be because of the hurt you are going to feel as the result of a relationship you haven't even had yet, with a person you haven't even met yet? And could this sense of danger be responsible for the negativity you are experiencing right now? This notion is both crazy and exciting in equal measure. How can effects come before causes? If our future is affecting our present, what does time mean? These are fascinating questions that place relationships and dating firmly within the realm of quantum physics.

ACTION:
How would Lieutenant Columbo spot a yes/no within online dating? He would simply look for contradictions within their narrative. For example, someone who is fresh out of a **relationship, but insists they are ready for a new one, is an obvious example. Or someone who says they are emotionally available but they look unhappy in all their profile photos.** *Or someone who states their desire to be with someone, while ensuring that they are perpetually busy or constantly travelling.*

The word *narcissism* derives from Greek mythology.

Narcissus was a man who fell in love with his own reflection in a pool of water. Narcissism as a modern personality trait is described by the Cambridge online dictionary as someone who displays "too much interest in and admiration for their own physical appearance and/or their own abilities." Such personalities have become the subject of much scrutiny in recent years, driven partly by the explosion of narcissistic behaviour displayed within social media. The narcissist — or *mirrorman/mirrorwoman* as I call them — has also become an archetypal villain within modern relationships — someone focused only on their own physical and emotional needs, who perpetually consumes the attention and energy of their partner, while never giving back. In general conversation, a narcissist is unlikely to say, "Anyway, enough about me, what about you?" The words narcissists use most often within their dialogue are, "me", "myself" and "I", while the ones they use the least are, "you" and "yourself". If you were to say to a narcissist, "I am thirsty," they are more likely to reply, "Me too," as opposed to, "Let me get you a drink."

Imagine a conversation with a narcissist. It might go something like this:

You: "I just bought a new cat."

Narcissist: "Oh, I've got a cat. My cat loves me. Whenever I come home and sit down, it always jumps up on the sofa and snuggles up next to me."

What is missing from modern definitions of narcissism is the fact that most of them have no idea that they are narcissists. They chatter endlessly about themselves without realising it, and would be surprised, if not offended, if you were to point it out to them. This entirely makes sense, because if narcissists were self-aware they probably wouldn't be narcissists in the first place. If you have trouble recognising one, or you want to find out if you are one, you can consult the Narcissistic Personality Inventory, a non-clinical means of measuring narcissism as a personality trait, devised in 1979 by psychologists Robert Raskin and Calvin Hall. The 10-minute test consists of 40 multiple-choice questions. Within online dating, narcissists can be easy to spot if you scan their approach work carefully. Visually, they tend to love selfies, especially those that depict them in contrived sexual poses. Their *Instagram* feeds — which many connect to their profiles — often reinforce this, with row-upon-row of images of themselves basking in their own beauty and sexuality. At no time in history have humans been more interested in their own self-image than now, in the age of the smartphone's digital camera — online dating sits at the apex of this new narcissism.

ACTION:

How do you spot a mirrorman/mirrorwoman? Their expression of extreme self-interest often manifests in what they choose to write in their profiles or within their messaging. Watch out for those who only appear to answer the questions you ask them, but do not ask you anything about yourself. Similarly, if on a date, be aware of those who talk constantly about themselves without referring back to you, or whom, if they do, quickly find a way to steer the conversation back to them.

3. Writing is truth

Scrutinising what online daters write is just as important in becoming a skilled emotional detective. The single biggest mistake people make within their summaries is not to write anything about themselves. *Tinder*, with its reputation for sex, is the app for those who don't like reading or writing. The experience is like visiting a library with no books, only pictures on its walls. I estimate that 80 per cent of the profiles I have seen on its UK site are empty of any written content. It is *Tinder*'s users, rather than the app itself, who are most culpable. It is a sign of a damaged society when, given the opportunity to speak within a democracy, humans choose silence. They choose to self-lobotomise, reducing themselves to the digital equivalent of shop window mannequins. Their human identity is erased, leaving only a stub — no speech, no story, no character — just image. They showcase *what they are, not who they are.*

It reminded me of the 1979 song, *We Don't Talk Anymore*, by Cliff Richard, which seems scarily, prophetically appropriate for these digital, non-verbal times. Remember the chorus?

It's so funny how we don't talk anymore.

The trend towards non-communication is of course reflected within wider society, from gamers who lock themselves away until they forget how to hold conversations, right through to married couples who have stopped communicating with one another. We all like to think of millennials as the generation who have grown up not knowing how to talk, but my generation, the over 40s and 50s are just as bad. In fact, we are worse, because we grew up with talking, but now online we have learned not to. Ultimately, who wants to date someone who has *nothing* to say, who offers no story? We all know that everyone has a story — that there is more behind the photographs, that there is content behind the eyes — and yet it is deliberately withheld. Therefore everyone is unknowable, and informed decisions impossible to make. In this, the so-called Information Age, information has become an anomaly. Instead, daters are forced to make snap judgements based on images, not only about attractiveness, but also other key measures such as trustworthiness, integrity or sense of humour. And of course, choosing a potential partner using only visual criteria will have a high failure rate. Very high.

After a while, scrolling through the endless carousel of wordless, anonymous imagery begins to take on an eerie quality, like the faces of missing persons from murder cases, where nothing is known about the victims. It is like a digital conveyor belt of John and Jane Does — cold cases with no clues, each one dismissible as they pass on by. The late Toni Morrison once said that, "What was driving me to write was the silence — so many stories untold and unexamined." The opposite is true within online dating, where the space for writing is left fallow. The well-worn phrase, "less is more", does not apply here. In this realm, less is less. The fact is, online, *if you write nothing, you are nothing*, because that is what you have chosen to be as your digital self.

Many online singletons fail to realise the key fact that a *dating profile is a resume*. In the same way that you would never send an empty employment resume to a recruiter, why would you post one on the Internet in your search for a partner? I have been amazed at some of the profiles posted by professionals that do not contain any language. I saw one recently on *Bumble*, from a woman who described her job as "head of communications". I have also seen the profiles of psychotherapists, PR directors, schoolteachers and lecturers, all without words.

By far the most common reason given by online daters

is that no one reads the copy anyway, and people, especially men, just swipe the faces they like. As a rationale for giving up your opportunity to tell your story, this attitude is lazy, or it suggests that you have given up. As a heterosexual man, I see this a lot online. Single females have been ground down by continuously abusive or flaky male behaviour, until they give up hope, and become cynical. In response, many resort to posting *skeleton profiles*, containing the bare minimum of detail. They are there, and yet not there. *They have ghosted themselves.* They have concluded that including some well-written text within their profiles will make no difference to anything, and so they have effectively abandoned their posts — but simultaneously they remain online, just in case — suggesting that somewhere within, hope remains. But the truth is that some people do read their text, and they are the ones to focus on, the readers of words. But ultimately, if only one person reads your narrative out of 1,000 people, it is still worth doing — even if that one person is you.

The fact that there are not many readers may actually be a good thing, as it becomes a way of narrowing the field. Choices can be further reduced by eliminating others who, instead of writing a bio, instruct us to "just ask". This is also lazy, as it shifts responsibility to the other party to start the dialogue about who you are, when really it should be you. *I can't be bothered to say anything about myself, so I want you to do the work, deal?* Would you want to date someone who shifts responsibility, rather than takes it on?

As online daters, we have allowed ourselves to be brainwashed by the apps into believing that pictures matter more than story, as opposed to a balance of both. Social media sites like *Instagram* reinforce this. There is also a certain narcissism at work when a dater is more consumed by what they look like than what they have to say about the person they seek. Some think that showing photos without text is somehow more intriguing, and will entice the curiosity of the viewer. But there is no intrigue when the majority of profiles adopt this position.

There are also emotional reasons why daters choose not to include written content. Many people, for whatever unknowable reasons, are not ready to reveal who they are. There is a blockage of some kind. As mentioned, roughly 80 per cent of female *Tinder* profiles I came across in the UK were empty of words. If we were to take this as an average, could this mean that 80 per cent of all single people online are not quite in the best place for the relationship they seek? Because if they were, would they not simply say so, enthusiastically, in writing? The idea that most daters are not ready to date is also suggested by the fact that we all know from our general experiences online, that the less complete any forms that we fill in are, the less effective they will be at achieving their objective. In the case of online dating, fully completed profiles are more popular than partially finished ones. Given this, the fact that most daters consciously choose not to complete their submissions is very telling.

ACTION
What does a profile without words imply about its author? Are they lazy, have they given up or are they not ready for a relationship? Whatever their reason for choosing silence, you must decide whether you seek a communicator or a non-communicator; someone who withholds information, or who puts it out there; someone who has given up on writing because

they think no one reads, or someone who keeps on trying.

Even when online daters do include text, there are often grammatical and spelling errors. In this regard, adults are often worse than schoolchildren. In class, kids are taught to check spelling and grammar before submitting their work, but within online dating adults regularly post text in which they have not done this basic step. This same person wouldn't tolerate errors within their work resume, but they are happy to do so within their dating profile. My thinking is, anybody who can't bothered to check their own work, maybe won't pay attention to other details within a relationship. As a writer, I have often been contacted by people with spelling and grammatical errors within their messages. I delete them instantly. I also delete those who communicate via rows and rows of emojis instead of words, which they expect me to look through and decipher.

For many who do write, and without errors or emojis, there are often other problems, such as unoriginality. After a few weeks online, the repetitive clichés within people's profiles became mind-numbingly boring — "I like good coffee, walks in nature, dinner with friends, meaningful conversations, cheese, red wine and *Netflix* box sets; just as happy going out as staying in; try not to take life too seriously; no ONS or hook-ups." It was as if they have all been written by the same person. I wanted to know everything *aside* from the fact that someone likes *Netflix* and cheese, which of course most of us do, including me. I yearned for something surprising, personal, or more insightful than this standard stuff.

As a writer I have learned to closely scrutinise words and their meanings, and to make decisions about which singletons may or may not be right for me as a result. Here is my personal list of the words and phrases I am generally wary of when I see them posted in dating profiles:

"Shopping/shopaholic". *(Consumerism is a bit of a turn off).*
"I am beautiful…." *(Narcissistic self-pronouncements? Nah.)*
"Smoker". *(I don't).*
"Atheist". *(I believe in Spirit).*
"Average/ordinary". *(Hello? I want someone extraordinary).*
"Busy". *("Busy" is a myth. You want something, make time).*
"Workaholic". *(See above).*
"I have no baggage". *(It is not human to not have baggage).*
"I am drama-free". *(See above).*
"I am looking for a gentleman". *(What is that? Something from a 19th century novel?)*
"I am looking for my prince charming/knight in shining armour". *(Fairytales? Really?)*
"I am a queen in search of my king". *(What? Royalty? I'm just a guy).*
"I am looking for a partner in crime". *(Bonnie & Clyde, yeah? You want a boyfriend or a criminal?)*
"I'm looking for someone to make me smile again". *(Prefer someone who is already smiling, thanks).*
"I'm looking for someone special". *(No, really? You're not interested in someone crap?)*
"Looking for someone to make me happy". *(That's your job).*
"I'm looking for someone who doesn't take life too seriously". *(Life* is *serious, look around).*
"Divorcing/getting divorced". *(Still married).*
"Newly-single/newly-separated/just divorced"
(Sounds emotionally unavailable).
"I travel a lot for work". *(Totally unavailable).*

"I live abroad". *(See above).*

"I live in a town outside London". *(Prefer not to travel for three hours to see you).*

"I am in London visiting". *(Do I look like a tour guide?).*

"I don't know what I'm doing online dating…" *(Really? Er, so…).*

"Want to know about me? Ask". *(Oh please. Why not just say something?).*

Some of you reading through my list may think I am being slightly harsh with some of my disqualifying terms, but it is good practice for all online daters to decide what their own linguistic boundaries are, so that they have some tools to quickly narrow the field and assess a person's suitability. There are no accidents in the language daters *choose* to describe themselves within their profiles. They reveal deep-seated truths that their authors may not be consciously aware of. For example, I read several profiles in which women in denial have described themselves as having "no baggage". How can this possibly be true? To say someone has no baggage is to say that they have never been negatively affected by anyone they've ever met — that they have not been altered by experience. Baggage is what makes us human, what makes us interesting, complex and difficult.

Another negative signal is thrown up whenever someone tells me within their profile text that they are "busy", or a "workaholic". This implies that they may not actually have time for the relationship they are advertising for. There is an implied contradiction between intention and availability. Imagine meeting someone for a first date, who said, "Hi, I'm Katherine, I'm *busy* most evenings and weekends." Not a great start — but if you reversed this language, and instead she said,

"Hi, I'm Katherine, I'm *free* most evenings and weekends," the perception is totally different, suggesting someone who is ready and available. There is a growing body of older daters, eager to get more out of the culture, who have now taken to closely examining text in this way. *Financial Times* journalist and schoolteacher Lucy Kellaway, who is single, 60 and online dating, insists that rather than scrutinising the photos on people's profiles, instead she examines "prose, hunting for signs of intelligence, culture and humour — a sifting process that is less likely to lead to dismal dates."

ACTION
Just as setting out your personal red lines is a very good way to eliminate undesirables and to narrow the field of choices, it is important to show flexibility in exceptional cases where you encounter someone amazing who appears to disobey your rigid rules. For example, I for one, always keep to my red lines, and never go against my principles. I would never date an atheist, or a person in a boring job — unless of course they were gorgeous, funny, smart and emotionally available.

Aside from daters who write nothing, or who write in clichés, or whose copy features spelling and grammatical errors, every now and again there are some amazing, standout examples of writing from single people who have mastered the art of effective communication. Here are two of my favourites:

"Looking for a co-pilot, not a passenger, or a captain."

This is one of the best opening lines I ever read on a woman's online dating profile. It says more in one sentence than many say in an entire paragraph. If you ever read a line this good in someone's profile, you can cut the chit-chat and go straight to marriage.

This is another good one:

"I am 5ft 1, slightly moody, but with a good heart."

This single line is packed with crucial information. Many men do not like short women, so she is upfront about that, as she is about the negative aspect of her character — her moodiness. Not many online daters confess their faults, but she is brave enough and has the self-awareness to put it out there. Then she finishes the sentence on a high, by telling us that she is of a kindly, generous disposition. The sequencing of information, starting off with the negatives, then ending on a positive, is excellent.

On the other hand, some of the things people write within their profiles make no sense whatsoever. I remember one person who offered this single line within her posting:

"Secret for my life."

What the heck does this mean? What is someone supposed to make of this intriguing nonsense?

This aside, the scariest thing I read was from a blonde heavy metal fan who wrote this:

"If crazy = genius, then I am a rocket scientist."

8

How To Create The Best Online Dating Profile (The 9 Steps)

I often hear online daters confess that they "didn't put much effort" into their profiles, or that when it comes to ways of improving them, that they "can't be bothered". I always think, *Well why the hell not?* If you are serious about finding a partner, shouldn't you be serious about your dating profile too? Admittedly, I was guilty of this kind of apathy when I first went online. I was annoyed at how much work was involved — selecting and editing pictures, plus writing a compelling description of myself and what I was looking for. It was like applying for a job. It seemed to take almost as much time as drafting a work resume and cover letter to an employer. But then I thought, isn't it right that it does actually take this amount of time? Isn't finding your potential life partner as important as finding that great job, if not more so? A job may only last until retirement age at best, but your soulmate, hopefully is for life — so shouldn't you give your profile the same, if not more attention than you would give your resume? Indeed, shouldn't it be as amazing as your resume?

In reality most are not. The average dater spends more time on their hair than they do on their profile. They are often hurriedly constructed, with poor quality photography, no text, or else badly scripted copy riddled with spelling and grammatical errors, or containing irrelevant information.

Many of these people then complain about not attracting the partners they seek, without acknowledging that they are in fact part of the problem. Just as a person would be eliminated from a job interview if they submitted an empty resume, or one containing spelling errors, why would a dater not expect the same treatment online? Many have yet to grasp that an online dating profile is a piece of marketing literature — perhaps the most important of your life.

Many singletons appear to have given up hope, abandoning their profiles like burned out cars in a parking lot, no longer tending to them, and yet still hoping to attract an amazing partner. What is the thinking here? Could self-sabotage be part of it? Deep down, perhaps their inner voice is saying:

If I make my online dating profile really, really amazing, it might increase my chances of finding a great partner. Shit, but then I might be happy. I'm not sure I could handle that.

If it is true that humans put the least amount of time into the things they value the least, what does it mean when on online dater only puts 10 minutes work into their profile, instead of 10 hours? If you are one of these people, ask yourself this:

Am I really ready for the relationship that I say I want?

This question, and others, are explored below in my definitive nine-step guide to how to create the best online dating profile:

1. Is This The Right Time?

This is the first question you should ask yourself before signing up to any dating apps. Many of us use online dating as a vehicle to recover from past relationships, when actually we are less than ready to be fully engaged with it. This can create confusion, both for you and for potential suitors. I first signed up just 10 weeks out of a six-year relationship, and this proved to be much too early. I hadn't spent enough time in the *healing zone*. Many single people go online much sooner than I did, when their personal circumstances are less than ideal. I have one friend who joined *Hinge* on the same afternoon she split from her long-term partner. During my time online I have been messaged by women who were in the middle of their divorces, and another who was six-months pregnant with a sperm donor baby. If you are in situations like these, be honest with yourself — are you in the right frame of mind to be online dating right now? If you are already online, but your profile contains only one picture, or images in which you appear to be hiding your face, or which contain no text, etc — the same question applies. Have you healed sufficiently from your previous relationship, or are you still harbouring feelings of anger, confusion or sadness about what happened? Are you emotionally available for a new encounter, or do you need to **do more work on yourself first?**

2. Understand The Game

If you decide that you are ready to sign up, you should do some homework about online dating first. Many people subscribe without getting any guidance about what to do or what to expect, and then they are sent reeling in horror after the negative effects of first exposure. Many of the mistakes first timers make when creating their profiles are simply due to the fact that they do not know the protocols. The fact that you are reading this book is a good start, but there are lots of online resources that can help too. Beware of asking friends for their view, as those for whom it has been unsuccessful are likely to offer negative conclusions that may put you off. The truth is, you will have to be prepared for the fact that you may have to fight your way through hundreds of trolls, damaged humans, liars, cheats, time-wasters, racists, misogynists, narcissists and adulterers, before you find the one who is the right for you — and this process may take a long time. New daters sign-up like naïve infantry, their expectations go unmanaged, and they crash into the fray completely unprepared for the ensuing social warfare. To succeed you might find it useful to think of it as a terrain, a battlefield in which you have to enter with your armour up and your eyes alert, and that you have to be fleet of foot to glide past the undesirables without absorbing their negative energies. It is not far away from being a warrior in a video game, fighting your way past hordes of ghouls and other monsters in a cross-country quest to find your beloved.

3. Choose Your App(s) Carefully

There are a plethora of options catering to every niche and desire. *Forbes* estimates there are currently 8,000 worldwide, with 1,000 new launches per year. *Tinder* is the market leader, but it may not necessarily be right for you. Its reputation is that it is the go-to app for hook-ups and one-night-stands, and many men in particular still use it with this in mind. Consequently its focus is primarily aesthetic and sexual, and users tend not to read or post wordy profiles. Many female *Tinder* users complain about this, and being constantly propositioned for sex, when they might be better off on another app with a different focus. However, what does make *Tinder* hard to ignore is that it has more users than any of its rivals (an estimated 50 million worldwide).

Specialist sites have smaller user numbers but gain from being highly targeted. They offer niche services to daters based on religion, age, ethnicity, occupation, political persuasion and even celebrity. In 2016 *RAYA* launched, catering exclusively for the famous, as well as high-profile media executives. It is an exclusive club, and would-be members have to apply and be accepted before joining. Demi Lavato, Amy Schumer, Drew Barrymore and Kelly Osbourne have been reported as subscribers. Swiss dating app, *Once* is devised for those tired of mass swiping, and instead uses a team of in-house matchmakers to select a small number of options, which they send out to singles each day at noon.

If you have specific circumstances that you want to disclose to daters upfront, apps that do not allow users to write their own narratives, such as *Hinge*, may not be the best option, although a good workaround would be to inform people during your messaging exchange instead. By contrast *Guardian Soulmates* is designed for very detailed and lengthy written profiles. Users have a total of 4,000 characters to write about themselves and what they are looking for. *eHarmony* also has an extended sign-up process. Both take a long time to populate, but the advantage is, because so much information is revealed upfront, it can result in more accurate matches, as well as allowing daters to progress to meeting much sooner, whereas *Tinder* requires a lot of preliminary texting after the matching process, due to the fact that their profiles are mostly empty. The less you know about someone, the more questions you have to ask. This is an important consideration because things can soon gets tiring if you are communicating with several people at once.

Price is another consideration. Most apps operate a "freemium" model in which it is free to join, but then subscribers pay to access the full range of services. *Hinge* offers good value at £8.99/$12.99 per month to subscribe, whereas *Guardian Soulmates* is expensive at £32.00/$40.00 per month. *eHarmony* is even pricier at £38.99/$48.00 with a minimum sign-up period of six months, paid in advance. In-app purchases which boost the visibility of your profile can cost as much, or even more than a monthly subscription. *Tinder*'s *Super Boost* feature, which catapults your profile to the top position for three-hours during peak time, costs £38.99/$48.00 for each execution. If dating apps are increasingly seen as entertainment devices by many users, they appear to overpriced compared to other platforms. *Netflix* for example, charges just £8.99/$12.99 per month — significantly less than the majority of dating apps. Granted, they won't find you a partner, but they can guarantee you stress-free pleasure on a Friday night — which dating apps cannot do.

You should do your own research before choosing which app, or apps are best for you. When I started I signed up to four different options, including *Tinder*, allowing me to compare and contrast the various offers, after which I reduced it down to two. But remember, subscribing to more than one at a time increases your overall engagement time per day, and also the costs of any subscriptions.

4. Do It With A Friend

Creating your profile purely on the basis of your own

preferences and assumptions about yourself is a big mistake. Why? Because *you are not the target audience. You are not dating yourself.* Just because you like a certain photograph of yourself doesn't mean that it is the best image to use to attract your ideal partner. The pictures you post are of you, not for you. Instead, ask yourself, *what information does the person I am trying to attract want to see?* Would they prefer to see a photo of me looking happy or sad, for example? Would they prefer to see a picture of a beautiful sunset or a picture of my beautiful face? Seeking someone else's opinion on your content can be the difference between success and failure. Heterosexuals should choose a friend of the opposite sex who can offer a gender specific view, and whose opinion you trust. According to the *Pew Research Centre*, 22 per cent of American online daters have asked someone else to help them create or review or review their profile. Women are more likely than men to do so, but currently the numbers for both genders are still too low.

5. Create Winning Images
Don't settle for poor quality
In the age of high quality digital cameras on every smartphone, there is no excuse today for online daters posting poor quality imagery. Those who post blurry images, or those that are too dark to see their faces, or else their faces are cut off in the frame, etc, are doing themselves a disservice. If you can't be bothered to post good pictures of yourself, why should anybody be bothered to date you? Why not post images that make you look amazing? Won't this increase your chances of attracting someone amazing?

Don't take all your own pictures

When creating your profile, instead of taking multiple selfies, why not get a good friend to take some pictures of you instead? Select a few smart clothes, use natural light and have some fun. They will turn out better than selfies, which have now become a sad cliché. Alternatively, you could go one better and hire a professional photographer. This shows daters you are serious, and willing to go the extra mile to present yourself in the best way possible. Aim to get as many different portraits and body shots as you can within the allocated time. Remember, the better the pictures, the better the impression. Whenever I suggest this idea to my online dating friends, many are resistant, considering it a step too far, but the process doesn't have to be wildly expensive. There are many headshot photographers online who specialise in portrait and body shots for actors, who you can book for around £200 ($250). The expense is also justified by the fact that, beyond dating, having a good set of pictures is always useful, as you can give copies to friends and family.

Upload lots of pictures

A 2016 study by Queen Mary University, London revealed that the number of images a user posts on *Tinder* has a notable impact on levels of engagement. Women who increased their photos from one to three experienced a 37 per cent increase in matches. With male profiles the increase was even more dramatic, with engagement levels spiking by 500 per cent with three images. *Tinder* allows users to upload up to nine photographs, while *Bumble* and *Hinge* allow for six. Use as many as you can, providing that you have the right quality of imagery.

Know the pictures you should never post

These are the ones that generally obscure the information a potential match wants to know about you, or else presents off-putting cliché's or character traits. For example, you may think you look super cool in designer sunglasses, but they hide your face, preventing people from seeing you, and so shouldn't be featured at all. "Hiding your face doesn't just make you look sketchy. It also means you miss the chance to convey to other users that you're trustworthy and friendly," says online dating sociologist Jessica Carbino. A good way for heterosexuals to assess the do's-and-don'ts for themselves is to log on to the apps and view the profiles of those of your own gender. In this way you can see the worst clichés people use. Here is my summary checklist of the images you should never include in your online profile:

General

You in narcissistic mirror selfie (with phone in shot).

You in flesh-revealing mirror selfie with your head cut off.

You and your best friend (who is better looking than you).

You with best friend in every photo, so we don't know who is who.

You in shots with other people in which their faces are scratched out.

You with your ex (or someone who could be mistaken for them).

You with your ex cropped out of the photo (but with their severed hand or face still in shot).

You with a celebrity you met socially or at a work function.

You and your children who have not consented to being shown.

You and babies or young children who are not yours, but may be mistaken for yours.

You as a baby.

You with childish Snapchat filters.

You sticking your tongue out.

You drunk or stoned or both.

You wearing sunglasses, goggles or hats in most or all of your photos.

You skiing with goggles on.

You in shots where you are too far away to be seen.

Proverbs, wise sayings, sunsets and images of nature.

Pictures of your feet, legs, torso, back of your head or anything without your face in it.

Pictures of you from the past, looking younger than you do now.

You looking sad or angry.

You wearing culturally inappropriate fancy dress — Native American headdresses, hijabs, Hitler outfits, etc.

Men

You proudly brandishing a big fish you've caught.

You hugging a sedated tiger on some exotic holiday.

You with your material possessions – yacht, car, motorbike, mansion.

Your bare torso in narcissistic mirror selfie at the gym.

You in selfie in a public lavatory.

You holding a gun, knife or other weapon, real or fake.

You signing the wedding register with your then wife.

Dick pics.

Women

You in narcissistic mirror selfie wearing sexually revealing clothing.

You with long hair covering or obscuring your face.

You wearing heavy make-up in every photo.

Know the pictures you should post

The best profile photo a dater can post is one in which they are smiling, with their face forward and their eyes to camera.

Smiling always works. Humans are hardwired to respond to it. It says, *Hi, I am open, I am friendly, I am happy*. Unsurprisingly, in research, straight-to-camera images yield the highest engagement. "People who face forward in their profile photo are 20 per cent more likely to be swiped right," says Carbino. In her research, she analysed 12,000 photos from the profiles of US online daters, to determine what factors help someone find a match. Another of her takeaways was that those who wear bright colours and patterns in their photos attract more positive swipes. Be aware that these rules are not absolute. There are many creative images for example, in which daters are not smiling or looking to camera, but the artistry within the composition elevates their impact.

Most daters also want to know your body type. A profile that only contains headshots feels suspicious, as if there is an issue with revealing the rest. The viewer wants to know — are you full-figured, slim, athletic? Include a full-length body shot, either standing or reclining. You don't have to be semi-nude, you could simply wear a well-fitted outfit. This also allows you to show off your fashion sense, which is also important to many people. Alternatively, if you want to show a prospective match what you look like with very little clothing, a beach shot of you in a bikini (or trunks if you are male) will appear more natural than a mirror selfie.

You could also populate your photographs with background objects, or "conversation starters" as they are better known. Daters are always looking for ways to start a chat with those they connect with, and will often study the details of photos for clues and ideas. In July 2018, Los Angeles comedian and writer Hana Michels, posted an image of herself on *Tinder* that was taken in her bathroom. In the background, male viewers commented on the direction in which her toilet roll was facing within its holder. This small detail provided an introductory talking point for potential dates. Creating photographs with deliberately planted objects of interest is a fun way to illicit responses. An elaborate pair of earrings, an eye-catching book cover or an image from a television in the background can all provide good hooks.

The option to upload video is a recent addition to dating app profiles, and one that very few have so far taken up, as the format is more revealing, and relies on an element of performance that many are uncomfortable with. However, they have amazing standout appeal compared to photographs, and can convey a truer sense of your physicality and sexuality. People also linger for longer with video. A study by *Instagram* revealed that video posts receive *twice the engagement of photographs*. Within online dating, this could mean you increasing the number of positive swipes you get. If you decide that video is for you, keep your posts short — 10 seconds or less — and choose a theme which shows you being funny or creative. Lastly, ensure that you are smiling before you hit record, so the first frame of your video captivates the viewer's attention.

When you have all your images ready, place your best one first in your profile. It sounds obvious, but many daters overlook this, and instead sequence their photos in reverse order — the worst ones first. Always introduce yourself with a headshot. A close-up of a face carries more impact than a full-body shot, or an image in which you are standing very far away on top of a mountain. With so many people now online dating, the assessment process has speeded up, with daters making snap judgements based on your opening photo, and so it is foolish to presume they will scroll through all of them first. Remember also that when your profile photo is sent to a prospective match and sits there in the queue with the others, the app will select to show your first picture, and so if it lacks impact it will be lost amongst the others. If you don't know what your strongest image is, ask a friend for help. *Tinder*'s algorithm actually makes the decision for you, by automatically showing your images according to popularity, but not all dating apps have this feature.

To recap, here is a summary of the principles for creating a great visual profile.

Smile.
Start with your best picture (smiling headshot).
Wear bright colours.
Include a body shot or two.
Create conversation starters within your photos.
Do not take all your own pictures.
Use video.

6. Write Something
Queen Mary University's research into *Tinder* revealed that 36 per cent of all accounts contained no written biography, and of those that did, the majority consisted of only 100 characters (from a maximum 500). These figures varied according to gender, with 42 per cent of female profiles being empty, and 30 per cent of men's. The higher female number is attributed to the fact that women tend to attract matches regardless of whether or not they include text, as men are more visually focused, whereas conversely, more men contribute copy because women are less aesthetically focused. Overall, not

including a written accompaniment to your images is a mistake. It suggests you have nothing to say for yourself, that you have no story, that you are lazy, apathetic or even arrogant. Why would anyone want to date someone who chooses silence over expression? The justification often used — that no one reads the profiles anyway — is a poor excuse for being silent about how amazing you are. Simultaneously, in saying nothing, you are in fact saying something — which is that you wish to be judged visually — and only this way. *You are volunteering to be objectified.* But when this judgement comes, daters are offended by it, despite the fact that they are the architects of their own mute state.

Having no text also means there is no conversation starter other than your pictures, which means that some singletons will not message you, as they don't know what to say. "A lot of individuals need to have fodder to make conversation," says Carbino. "It's very difficult for people sometimes to put themselves forward and try to make that first move." For those who do message you, the less you write about yourself and your circumstances, the more preliminary questions they will then have to ask before they can progress onto whether or not you like art house cinema. This slows the whole process down, unnecessarily extending the number of texts exchanged in order to evaluate whether or not to meet. And if any of the basic facts disclosed within those first messages do not match up with a person's preferences, they may not be a match anyway, in which case you have both wasted your time.

Your written profile should be a mix of *character, situation and requirements* — character is, "I am a kind, loving person"; situation is, "I live in the countryside with two kids aged five and eight"; requirements are, "I am looking for a tall, compassionate man who seeks a long-term relationship". When scripting your narrative, make sure you also answer the basic questions a mature dater wants to know. For example, if you are single parent, it is not enough to say you have children who live with you — state their ages, gender and how much time off you have from them during evenings and weekends. On the other hand, if you do not have children, state whether you do or do not want some in the future. Also state your height, where you live and other basic info someone would like to know about you.

Avoid clichés when revealing your hobbies and interests. Stating how much you enjoy red wine, cheese, country walks, travel and *Netflix* is bland, because everyone says it. Instead, think about what is different or special about you. Avoid the overuse of emojis instead of actually writing copy, as this can look lazy and immature. The written word, although it takes longer to craft, carries more emotional power than symbols. Think about what resonates more — someone who sends you a picture of a heart, or someone who writes, "I love you." Also be aware of using off-putting language such as swear words, or adjectives like "busy" or "workaholic". Do not use your precious allocation of words simply to rant bitterly about your negative experiences at the hands of the app's abusers — instead focus on what is great about you. Finally, check your copy for grammar and spelling errors. My thinking is, anybody who can't even be bothered to check their own work, maybe won't pay attention to other details within a relationship.

If you wish to avoid the non-writers within dating apps, set a rule never, never to swipe right on an empty profile. This is a good way to narrow the field and to focus instead on those who are ready to talk and reveal. You may also want to weed out those who have not read your own profile text. You can do this by putting a note at the very end of your written piece, asking the person to write, "YES" as the first word of their response after you have matched, indicating that they have read your text. Whoever doesn't write "YES" has not bothered to read your intro, and so you can delete them if you wish, before getting into a time-consuming dialogue.

I worked out that personally, when on *Tinder* I swipe right on only approximately four per cent of the women on the app, mainly because their profiles are incomplete, and/or I don't find them attractive. But the decision to reject those with empty profiles does get challenged when you come across someone who is *unbelievably gorgeous*. I have weakened many times during such moments, my finger hovering over their image, knowing that I should swipe left, but somehow not being able to. But in the end, the same rule applies — it doesn't matter how beautiful a person is, if they have written nothing, they are saying nothing.

Creating a complete profile is worth it in the end. According to *Bumble* fully completed bios with words and pictures are 27 per cent more popular than partially finished ones. The Queen Mary University study reported that female bios with text received 58 per cent more matches compared to empty ones, while the equivalent male profiles received a *400 per cent* spike. So, you are letting yourself down if your dating profile is incomplete. There is little point in posting a sub-standard bio, and then complaining that you can't find anybody decent. *Fix yourself first, before complaining about the externals.*

Here are two of my own written profiles. This first one is from *Guardian Soulmates*:

Who I'm looking for

Looking for a	Woman
Aged between	39 and 55
In my own words	An autonomous force, positive soul, someone funny, sexy, smart, fit, healthy. Emotionally available (but really though).
	What I'm not looking for? A woman with a hairy back and no teeth. Anyone who is not over their ex, or their ex ex, or their ex ex ex (you get the picture).

About me

Height	6' 1" (185cm)
Hair	Shaven
Eyes	Brown
Body type	Athletic
Relationship status	Single
Relationship sought	Let's see what happens; Long-term relationship
Has children?	Yes, not living with me
Wants children?	Maybe
Star sign	Aries
In my own words	Hi there. A quick summary:

1. I've had a chequered career, from modelling to architecture. Today I am a writer of books.

2. My parents were working class Nigerians who came to London in 1961. I am one of eight (no. 5).

3. Disgusting habit – picking food out of my back teeth in restaurants (without putting my hand over my mouth first). Toothpicks are my best friends.

4. I am badly short-sighted, so without my lenses or glasses everyone is a blurry beauty.

5. I have a keen sense of my own issues and vulnerabilities, so if you hang with me I'll open that box, so you know who you're dealing with.

6. I like dancing naked after I come back from running, just before I jump in the shower. (Just the one tune).

7. I don't like mobile phone zombies (or indeed any kind of undead dead person).

8. I only listen to Radio 4. In fact, I'd like a Radio 4 radio, that doesn't get any other station. (Alright, maybe 6 music too).

9. I love a good restaurant – but nothing beats fish 'n' chips by the sea with an amazing woman.

This second example is the text I used on *Bumble* and *Tinder*.

6'1, made in Nigeria, born in London; got a big-mouthed smile wider than Julia Roberts's; into sports, the arts and walking in nature under big skies. I am short-sighted too, so you will look great forever.

Would love to hear from you if your values are emotional and spiritual, rather than material; ideally slim, fit, healthy, tallish, smart, funny, non-smoker, living in London. I am 52, with a 23-yr-old son. Wordless profiles I generally swipe left.

7. Protect Your Identity

Due to the free availability of digital information about almost everyone, first dates are often not "first", because the person you are meeting has already Googled you, and therefore has some prior knowledge of who you are. Therefore much of the mystery and intrigue of meeting someone new has now evaporated, and daters have lost control of the ability to let their stories unfold in their own telling. This is particularly true of people like me who work in the media, and therefore have a bigger online footprint than others. I once went on a date in which the person I was meeting had already Googled me and bought one of my books, and was halfway through reading it by the time we sat down. I want to be valued first for *who I am, not what I am*, and I felt robbed of the opportunity to introduce myself from scratch, to reveal myself first as a person, before my profession and its products. When constructing your profile, if you wish to retain control of your personal narrative, do not give out enough information about yourself to allow someone to Google you in advance. Do not use your full name on your profile, the specifics of your profession, the exact place where you work or the name of the company.

8. Do Not Lie

In the world of online dating many people are concealing or lying about something. It could be that they are not really single, or not really divorced, or that their profile photos are 10 years old. According to Catalina Toma, Assistant Professor of Communication Arts at the University of Wisconsin-Madison, 81 per cent of singles misrepresent their height, weight or age in their profiles. *eHarmony* contend that US women mostly lie mostly about their age, while men lie about their jobs or how much money they earn. In my case I lied about my age. I stated that I was 48 as opposed to 52, my actual age. I did this for marketing purposes. People say that I actually look nearer 40, but the reason I wanted to come in under 50 is because according to research, women's view of men's desirability peaks at 50, and so women in their 40s tend not search for men beyond that age, and so I was not appearing in their results.

What is crucially important in all cases in which anyone lies, is to tell the truth before you meet. I usually insert my real age within my written profile, but not all apps have this facility, and so alternatively, as soon as I start messaging, I reveal it there, with a brief explanation about why I concealed it. This gives the other person the opportunity to make a decision before we meet, given the key facts. What you should never do is arrive on a date with crucial information undisclosed. The misguided thought process for liars and concealers is always the same. The narrative runs something like this:

If I can just get in front of them, if they can just see what

> *a great, amazing, funny, interesting and sexy person*
> *I am, they will forgive me for the fact that I am married*
> *with children, and actually 5'2' instead of 6'1'.*

I recently learned of an incident in which a female friend embarked upon a first date with a man she believed to be black, but when he arrived he was actually Indian. The conversation went like this:

"Are you Susan?" asked the man.

"Yes. Who are you?"

"I'm Brian."

"What? You're Brian?"

"Yes. Brian."

"But, I thought you were a black man?"

"Yeah, I know. But I am a person of colour."

"But...you're not the man in the dating profile."

"True."

"So, whose pictures were they?"

"A friend's."

"So you lied. This is fucking ridiculous."

"Wait, but I am brown."

"But you're not black, are you?"

"No, but I am not white either."

"For fuck's sake, you are not the man I saw online. That's who I thought I was meeting."

"I know. But I'm here now. We may as well have a drink."

Daters like Brian withhold the truth because of the fear they'll be rejected, but this seldom works, because once the truth comes out after meeting, the person will probably reject you anyway, only this time with the added annoyance that you lied, and they have wasted their time coming to meet you. I once made the mistake of going on a first date with someone without revealing my real age in advance. When I finally told her, her face changed, and I knew she was annoyed. She was in her mid-forties, and still wanted to have a child, and I was too old for her liking. I felt bad that I had not been more upfront, and vowed to myself never to do it again.

9. Run Tests

Albert Einstein is famously credited with the quote, "The definition of insanity is doing the same thing over and over again, but expecting different results." This is exactly the situation with many profiles. People create their dating resume once, but never think to revise it thereafter, despite the fact that it may not be attracting the matches they desire. I know daters whose profiles have not changed since the very first one they posted, some years prior. How do they know whether or not it is optimised? No one can assume that once they've posted their images and text, that is the end of the story, and they can simply sit back and do nothing else.

Your profile should never be static. Dating profiles are marketing documents, and marketing campaigns are often pre-tested on their target audience, to see which ones they respond to best. You should do the same thing with your profile. When you have prepared it, instead of sitting back on your laurels, try running tests on your photography and text. Each week or two, try uploading a new lead photo, and see what effect it has on who approaches you. Try a different hairstyle, an outfit change or a different smile. Look again at your filter selections, or answer a different set question. Alternate your written summaries also. Anyone who doesn't work their material regularly is potentially losing out on great matches. But be aware that having a profile that requires constant tendering can be exhausting, and so regulating your usage is key.

*

If you find yourself resisting these nine recommendations, ask yourself why. If you hear yourself saying that you, "can't be bothered" with all this effort, consider whether or not you are totally committed to finding a partner at this moment in your life. You may be feeling fed up, jaded and disillusioned with online dating, but these feelings will only push you further away from taking positive action. We are all aware that Internet dating can be a horrible experience, but how will you find the one you want if you give up now?

9

The Protocols

When you have set up your online dating profile and are ready to go, before you begin, you should make yourself aware of the behavioural rules that govern online dating. It is an oversight that the service providers themselves do not promote a clear set of best practice guidelines and rules of engagement *within the apps themselves*. All the crucial information is hidden on their websites and on *YouTube*, where no one bothers to look, and so users just download the apps and go. As a result, ill-informed singletons stumble through the process, making bad mistakes when creating their profiles and engaging with users. The overall experience can leave many feeling emotionally traumatised, depressed or with low self-worth. Divorced singles are particularly prone to error, as typically they have not dated for anything up to 30 years, and so are unfamiliar with its new protocols.

Establishing behavioural guidelines for online daters is critical simply because the rules of engagement online are different to those offline. When we refer to the online realm as "a world", this description is quite accurate, in that it is still an essentially lawless place — like a town without a sheriff. And whenever a sheriff is away, humans act up. Transgressions that people can go to prison for offline, such as defamation or indecent exposure, routinely go unpunished online. Today a man can send a dick pic to a woman and face no censure, but if he were to expose himself to her in this way out in the real world, he could face prosecution. A criminal online is not necessarily a criminal offline. The two worlds do not meet, despite being occupied by the same humans. Centuries of culture have established the rules of social etiquette that we all expect and live by, but online no one owes you anything — not courtesy, not integrity, not politeness, not reliability, not even the truth. Rudeness, racism, misogyny — all the things society suppresses — seep out like digital pus. The Internet proves that modern humans have yet to evolve beyond these abuses, and that the only thing controlling them is the possibility of adverse public reaction or legal consequences.

In some cases abusers are brought to account for their digital misdemeanours. There was one such occasion in 2012, when Liam Stacey, a 21-year-old biology graduate from Swansea in Wales, was jailed after posting a series of offensive and racist tweets after black professional footballer Fabrice Muamba, who played for Bolton Wanderers, suffered a cardiac arrest on the pitch in the middle of an FA Cup quarter-final tie. Initially it was believed that he had died. Shortly afterwards Stacey posted on *Twitter*: "'LOL, Fuck Muamba. He's dead.'" His tweet quickly drew reactions across the network. Stacey hit back at black people who criticised him, calling them "wogs" and telling another to, "go pick some cotton". Users reported him to the police, who arrested him the day after.

In court the jury heard how, following his tweets, Stacey tried to claim that his *Twitter* account had been hacked. It also transpired that he'd attempted to delete his account as well. When interviewed, he claimed that he was drunk at the time he'd posted the offensive comments. He told police: "I don't know why I posted it. I'm not racist and some of my friends are from different cultural backgrounds." In sentencing, district judge John Charles told Stacey: "You committed this offence while you were drunk and it is clear you immediately regretted it. But you must learn how to handle your alcohol better." Curiously, alcohol is known to have many side-effects, but transforming someone into a racist is not one of them. Stacey sobbed throughout the hearing and held his head in his hands when sentenced to 56 days in jail. He was led away in handcuffs. Despite cases like this the racial abuse of black footballers on social media continues to this day.

What is fascinating about Stacey's case is that he did not appear to recognise his racist self — his digital alter ego. It was as if his character had split into two — the physical Stacey and the digital Stacey. The advent of the Internet means that everybody now manifests these two branches of their personality. Both entities are part of one whole, but express themselves differently. The digital avatar is the more outspoken, cruel, racist, homophobic, misogynistic, selfish side of ourselves, and the one we are least familiar with, day-to-day. Nowhere is this disconnect between the physical self and its digital alter ego more marked than within Internet dating. As well as offering ways for single people to connect, the apps are a place where abusers go to misbehave, in ways that would not be tolerated within society. The digital self who communicates via dating apps will invariably not behave in the same way as the individual who turns up for the date. A man who sends a picture of his penis to a woman online would not introduce himself to her in this way face-to-face — and ironically, he would be offended to learn if another man had sent such an image to his own sister or his mother.

Unwitting single people sign up for online dating, expecting digital avatars of its users to behave in the "decent manner" they have become accustomed to in real life, and then they reel in shock when they do not. These abuses are examples of the *detached humanity* that has become a by-product of the virtual world. The further away we get from being in the presence of other humans, the more separated we become from our true selves. A similar thing happens within warfare. The higher the bombers fly in the sky, the further away they are from the faces of those they bomb, and so the easier it is to drop their payload. Distance makes humans callous. Within online dating, the less we know about people, the easier it is for us to abuse them or to dismiss them with a swipe of the hand.

This detachment is intensifying as more and more dating happens online. The landscape is becoming less of an exercise in escapism from analogue life, and more and more an entire experience of its own. There are vastly more singles available online than we will ever see in a bar, coffee shop or party, and so for many the experience is more exciting, more engaging and overwhelming than anything that occurs in real life. "Rather than going to a bar, you'll spend your evening going into virtual bars buying other avatars virtual drinks with your crypto-currency," predicts Daigo Smith, founder of dating app, *LoveFlutter*. It is too easy to forget within all this, that the game is being played with real chips — in other words, real people with lives and emotions who could potentially be hurt by its dehumanising effects. For this reason, all online daters should be aware, both of the key behavioural modes in play, as well as the correct protocols that should be observed to ensure minimum damage to all. So, with this in mind here is my list:

1. Running Multiples

The etiquette within online dating that everyone should keep uppermost in their minds is that everyone is *running multiples* — that is, viewing, connecting with, messaging or dating several suitors simultaneously. It is accepted practice that daters have a number of options in play at any given time. The corrupting thought process is, why focus on one person when there are so many to choose from? No individual matters when there is such an instant and constant supply of replacements. People come and go like the wind, and no one owes anybody the courtesy of following through on any initial interest. It is a brand new experience within dating that single people have access to such a large database of individuals all at once, and it has created dizzying new levels of greed and flakiness, with people constantly cancelling, ghosting or ignoring messages. A dater might have to run multiples for a long time before he or she gets one date they like, and who actually shows up. To achieve this, the approach adopted by the most eager men is simply to *binge swipe* — generating a higher probability for matches. But each time someone tries to connect with an online dater, the problem is that they are totally unaware of how many other suitors are doing exactly the same thing. The law of running multiples is this:

You never know how many people someone is assessing.

This is the reality of digital life — data is concealed.

Running multiples means that online daters often have trouble keeping track of the names of those they are assessing, especially when recounting their adventures to their friends over coffee. To address this, online daters create secret nicknames to help identify who is who. They are usually chosen to reflect some standout aspect of the person's character. I have heard daters referred to as, "Underfloor Heating Man" (he sold underfloor heating), "Porsche Man" (drove a car of the same name), and "Tricky Dick" (small penis). I also learned two nicknames different women had for me — "Silver Shoes", on account of the silver trainers I wore on our first date — and "Hat Man", because I wore a trilby in one of my profile photos. I was grateful not to be called "Dog Breath", "Dick Brain" or "Chipolata Dick" — three real examples disclosed to me by female daters.

2. Set Up Your Red Lines

All online daters should have a set of principles that govern the choices they make about who to connect with. It is easier and faster to filter out those who are not appropriate for you if you have some red lines set up. This is necessary because of the massive numbers that are online — you need a mechanism to eliminate, not accumulate. Your red lines should be personal to you, but there shouldn't be so many as to effectively disqualify everyone either. Balance must be maintained between being realistic and being too picky. Decide on the types of photography, writing or modes of behaviour you will or will not tolerate. One of my red lines is that if someone cancels a first date, there are no second chances — unless of course, there is a major reason — and by "major" I mean, like a tsunami. Some of my friends think my "one strike and you're out rule" is harsh, but I am looking for someone who follows through on their promises, and isn't flaky.

3. Bring Proper Chat

The quality of your introductory communication when you first match with someone is critical. What you say in this first message can determine whether or not you will receive a reply, or get ghosted. According to research by Queen Mary University, the average message sent by men on *Tinder* is only 12 characters long, and in 25 per cent of cases it is less than six, suggesting that men are beginning conversations with a short greeting, such as "Hello". This sort of introduction should be avoided. A woman is less impressed by this:

Hey what's up?

But more impressed by this:

Wow, you've got amazing eyes.

A short greeting is not much of a conversation starter. It implies that you lack imagination, are not a good communicator, and that there is nothing special about you. Here is a summary of introductory words and phrases you should never use:

Yo!
Hello.
Hi/Hi there.
Good morning/afternoon/evening.
What's up?
Hey.
How you doing?/ How are you?/How's it going?
What's happening?

Online daters often confess that the reason they use these short greetings is because they don't know what else to say. The obvious way to deal with this is to examine the person's photographs or their text and to pick something out to begin a conversation. It could be a particular item of clothing or an accessory she is wearing, or something within the background of an image, or one of the interests or hobbies she mentions. To not do this, and to use a greeting instead, is just lazy, and sends a message that you do not think the person is special enough to say something bespoke.

4. Embrace Baggage

Older singles who have experienced divorce, betrayal, adultery, abuse, abandonment, major illness, nervous breakdowns and so on, may come with a lot of what we refer to as "emotional baggage". This may be defined as, *the sum total of every experience we have had that we have chosen to manifest negatively in the present.* But baggage, in rendering us imperfect, is what makes us distinct, difficult and desirable. This is absent from Internet dating profiles. Instead, singles present facades of fictitious loveliness that imply that dating them will offer up a problem-free world consisting only of bliss. Vulnerabilities are muffled and concealed, as if somehow relationships don't come with issues attached. For example, no one writes, *I am a grumpy person*, or, *I suffer from depression*, or, *I am a single parent struggling to cope*, or indeed any truths that might, to use a phrase, "put people off" — but a prospective partner will find out soon enough — and then what?

I have read many Internet dating profiles in which people state that they "have no baggage", as if this is an amazing thing, whereas in reality it is impossible to be human without it. The term has now become a dirty word within contemporary culture — but it doesn't have to be. Think about it like this:

Baggage = life experience.

Compare both terms in a sentence to pitch to a prospective first date: *Hi, I'm Ben, I am single, and I have a lot of baggage.* Or, *Hi, I'm Ben, I am single, and I have a lot of life experience.* We are all defined by the things we have been through, and this should be an attraction when you are assessing who is right for you. Personally, I am a big fan of older women who have come through adversity, or who have devised positive strategies and coping mechanisms to counter emotional issues that remain present within their lives.

5. Distance Dating

Dating those who do not live in the same city as you can be difficult, as it means less availability, as well as having to contend with the travelling, which can be tiring and expensive. However, for those who do not have many options close to where they live, there is little choice but to look further afield. Alternatively, for those who are prepared to re-locate, distance presents no problem. If you match with someone who lives far away and you decide to proceed to a first date, remember *never to meet without video messaging first*. Because of the distance involved, it is crucial to get a feel for the person upfront, before anyone starts travelling large distances. This will safeguard against the potential for that horrible moment when you first meet someone who's travelled a long way, only to feel no spark at all for them.

6. How To Say Hello

A first date should be cheap and brief. If you are meeting after work during the week, this usually means evening drinks, which can quickly become expensive, depending on the number of weekly dates you go on. Instead, if you focus your dates on the weekends, you can meet for tea or coffee in the daytime. This is a good way to restrict your activity and not to overuse the apps. It is also cheaper, and easy to limit dates to one hour. This is the optimal time you should give another human being. Anything less feels disrespectful. It is also short enough to cut things off if you feel the person isn't for you. Set your timeframe before you meet. Say something like, "It would be great to meet you for coffee for an hour on Saturday at 12." You don't have to meet in a café either. I am a big fan of "walk-n-talk" first dates, where you grab a coffee and then stroll through a local park. Some people may find this easier than sitting across a table from a stranger and having to give them eye contact. First dates should not usually include a meal, unless you are getting on so well during the drinks phase that both of you feel comfortable extending it. Avoid anybody who insists on going straight to food first, without having met you. Keep in mind that there are still many men out there who think that if they pay for dinner and drinks, that the woman owes them something other than conversation.

Women may need to take extra precautions on first dates with men. Always try to meet in daylight in a public place, and never at their home or yours. Ensure you tell someone where you are going, who you are meeting, and what time to expect you back. If you seek hook-ups or one-night stands, and so decide to meet at their home or yours, you should still tell someone, as outlined. Whatever you are looking for from a date, always remember, if your *instinct* about a person is that they are somehow not right, trust that feeling, and avoid them.

7. How To Say Goodbye

Conclude all dates with those you feel are not right for you with a polite text, sent the day after. It is good practice to leave things for 24-hours, otherwise the rejection can feel too fast, as if you didn't give the person enough consideration. Here is a sample of one of my goodbye texts:

> *It was lovely meeting you last night. Thank you for taking the time out. Just to let you know, I didn't feel enough of a spark between us, and I thought it best to say so, rather than to ghost you, which I really don't like. I wish you all the best in your search.*

Although there is no way to reject someone without disappointing them or potentially hurting their feelings, it remains good practice to try and communicate rather than to just disappear. Think about how bad it feels when someone ghosts you, and so try not to do the same to others. Everyone within the online dating ecosystem has a responsibility to behave as well as they can toward their fellow human beings. If we all did this, all dating apps, and indeed the whole world, would be better.

8. When To Ghost?

Ghosting is one of the most hated practices within online dating. It occurs when someone begins a dialogue with you, and then abruptly disappears without explanation, leaving you feeling bemused, or even hurt. Like many cultural practices that have found their way online, ghosting began in the analogue world. People would go on first dates, and then afterwards one party would withdraw, never to be heard from again. Within the digital realm it is also worth remembering that many non-dating platforms also have ghosts, although they are seldom talked about in the same way. I have been ghosted on business networking platforms such as *LinkedIn* and the *Angel Investment Network* for example, where investors, employers and recruitment consultants routinely court entrepreneurs and those looking for jobs, and then, for reasons unspecified, change their minds and disappear in a puff of digital smoke.

Many older people think of ghosting as something that misguided young people do to each other, as they regard them as less mature and less communicative than us mid-lifers — but this is incorrect. I have been ghosted by professional women in their forties and fifties, and on one particular occasion by an eminent London surgeon with three children — hardly an impetuous millennial. Being ghosted hurts because it leaves the recipient with a mouthful of unanswered questions. Why did they leave? What did I do? Am I not as lovely as I thought? Am I an arsehole? Ghosting makes you question your character. We all think of ourselves as nice people — until we get ghosted — and then suddenly we're not so sure.

There are three reasons why online daters do it:

1. They are not good communicators.
2. They are not really available, and only seek to chat.
3. They were put off by something you wrote.

Item three is widespread. If you've ever been ghosted after exchanging a series of texts, the clues will invariably be somewhere within your exchange of dialogue, usually at the end. You may have cracked a joke they didn't like, or made an inappropriate comment, or even simply stated your height, which may not have been what they were looking for. When I first began online dating, I ghosted people who sounded boring, or who sent me sloppy messages riddled with typos, or said things I didn't like. I recall ghosting one woman who asked me for my full name, so she could Google my professional profile before deciding if I was worthy. On another occasion I ghosted someone on *Bumble* after her answer to just one question. She contacted me with this intro:

"Hey! What's your favourite thing to do after work?"

I replied, "I'd love to go swimming in a warm ocean, then drink rum-on-the-rocks while sitting on the sand. What about you?"

24-hours later she responded, "I don't know really. Anything outdoors I guess."

Her answer to her own question was so weak, after having had plenty of time to think about constructing a good response, that I decided I was no longer interested. It would have been inappropriate of me to tell her that I was cutting our dialogue short because she was boring, and so I just ghosted her.

But the culture is cyclical — I have ghosted people, and I have been ghosted in return — so everything evens out in the end, right? I have altered my view on this. I now think, instead of ghosting, communications should be concluded with a short, polite goodbye, without going into detail about your reasons. To say, "I don't think we are quite matched," is more respectful than to ghost them. But is there ever a time when ghosting is good? The answer is yes, whenever someone is rude or abusive. In these cases, ghosting is like a punishment, like someone receiving a digital slap, a little stinger.

I once encountered a woman on *Hinge* whom I noticed wore a different set of earrings in each photo. I commented on this detail in my opening text to her. In her response she was very impressed that I had noticed, but then she asked what I did for a living. I replied that the answer was stated in my profile, which she obviously had not read. I considered it rude that after my attention to detail with her earrings, that she showed none for me. So I ghosted her. On another occasion I was contacted by a 42-year-old, art-loving management consultant with two grown-up children. Our intentions appeared to be aligned, and after a very promising exchange of texts we agreed to meet. I then offered her some dates, which she ignored for three days, so I ghosted her too.

The temptation for many in such instances is, instead of ghosting, to bite back, get into disputes or argue. But how many times can you do this before you become jaded and mentally exhausted? Ask yourself this: *I only have so much energy to put out there — where should I direct it?* To stay engaged consumes more emotional energy and keeps you in negative mode for far longer than simply severing the digital umbilical cord of your mutual connection. It is always better to *detach than to attach*. Bowing out gracefully engenders a better feelgood factor than battling with someone. Your role is not to try and fix a stranger's problems as you see them online. This is their journey, and your "truth" may not be theirs. The world cannot survive if we are all sniping at each other, so make your stand.

9. Respond To Messages
When I first began online dating, I would ignore women on

Guardian Soulmates who messaged me, if I didn't find them physically attractive. I didn't care that I was penalising them for something they had no control over. But then I quickly changed my mind after other daters did the same thing to me. To be ignored is one of the worst things humans can do to one another. Once I'd experienced how it felt to be sidelined after taking the time to write a well-crafted message, I decided to alter my behaviour. Instead, I started writing back to them, thanking them for taking time to write, before politely saying that I didn't think we matched. Most wrote back to say how great it was to get a reply, even if it wasn't the one they'd hoped for, and how unusual it was for anyone to bother. Through these interactions I came to learn how much power we all have in contributing to the sense of wellbeing of others. If we all set out to make each daily contact with people yield positive rather than negative results — in effect, to *use our power wisely* — the world would be a very different place.

All daters should consider writing back to those who take the time and trouble to write to them first. Finding someone attractive should not be a qualifying condition. However, if you are one of those lucky people who receives a high volume of messages, replying to all of them will not be feasible, so instead it may be better to respond to as many as you feel able to, and also not the messages that are abusive in nature.

10. On The Bench

The opposite of responding to those who connect with you is called benching. It occurs after matching, when someone keeps a dater on ice on the sidelines, without communicating with them. But despite its connotation with sports, once a dater is on the substitutes bench, they seldom get to "play". In the end, they get deleted. Many women who still want the man to make the first move get annoyed about being ignored in this way. I have read a number of complaints within women's online profiles in which they say things like, *Why bother swiping right if you're not going to fucking say anything?*

For women like this the probability of getting benched is high because, according to the Queen Mary University study, 63 per cent of messages sent by men on *Tinder* happen within the first five minutes of the match taking place, but the figure is only 18 per cent for women, suggesting that they tend to hang back and wait for men to respond first, which is risky, because they might not. The learning here for women is, if a man doesn't respond to you quickly after being matched, he is unlikely to. It is in a woman's interest therefore, to strike first.

Benching is also the result of the fact that large numbers of men tend to swipe right indiscriminately, as it is harder for them to secure matches, and then they do not follow up once they occur. "Many male users 'like' in a relatively non-selective way and post-filter after a match has been obtained," says Gary Tyson, who led the Queen Mary study. "This gaming of the system undermines its operation and likely leads to much frustration." Indeed, it is impossible for an online dater on the receiving end of this to know why they've been benched. The person may have changed their mind about you, having looked again, or they may simply be a narcissist who loves collecting, or else they could be busy running multiples and have just forgotten about you. None of these will make you feel good, and speculating on the reasons why changes nothing, and so it is better to accept the reality and move on. However, if your profile is not as good as it could be, this could be a factor in why it happened, and if so, you may want to consider improving it.

11. Understand Beauty

The attention given to beauty is greatly magnified within online dating. The most attractive women are its most passive operators, never having to reach out to anyone, as all the online traffic comes to them, sometimes in torrents of hundreds of messages per day. Sociologists from the University of Michigan research into online dating, which analysed the habits of 186,000 participants, reported that the most popular person in the study, a 30-year-old woman living in New York, received a staggering 1,500 messages during the month of the research — the equivalent of one message every 30 minutes, 24-hours-a-day. Because women like this receive the highest volumes, men who try to connect with them are unlikely to receive a response. Each man is in fact waiting in a very large and invisible digital queue. Another reason why the response rate is so low is because less attractive daters aim high in contacting these beauties. The Michigan study found that both men and women pursue partners who are on average 25 per cent more desirable than themselves. According to the research, the bigger the gap in desirability between two daters, the less likely the receiver is to reply. The best chance of receiving a response from them is to ensure that you only message them during peak periods when they are most likely to be active on the site — in other words, daily commuter hours, plus Sunday's and Monday's.

But life for the most attractive is not all rosy. The sheer volume of communications they receive is so overwhelming that what should be fun for them suddenly becomes hard work. Also, continually receiving such high volumes can render them more cynical about men, because amongst those numbers there will inevitably be many communications from abusers who send them dick pics, use offensive language or otherwise behave in an inappropriate manner.

12. Do Not Lie, Please Do Not Lie

As well as not lying within your profile, as outlined in the previous chapter, you should also avoid doing so within your subsequent messaging. This is the place to disclose anything important that you did not mention within your profile. If you are married, if you are older or shorter than you've stated, or anything else like this, say it here — *tell the whole truth and nothing but the truth*. It is your last chance before you step out of the door to meet them. The critical thing is for the person you are about to encounter to have all the relevant information about you *before you meet*.

13. Don't Be Funny

Humour is a big part of what makes a person desirable, but when should you show it? When you initially match with someone there is no way of knowing what their sense of humour is, and so I always think it is wise at first to be respectful, polite and complimentary, but not to crack jokes until you are absolutely sure about what they find funny. What you think is hilarious may be offensive to them. I once exchanged messages with a woman who had not been Internet dating for long, and after a while she confessed that in terms of a date, that I would be her first. I joked that this meant that she was a virgin. She didn't find this funny, and so she ghosted me.

14. Ignore Those You Know

As more and more single people sign up for Internet dating within specific cities, the greater the likelihood that you will come across the profile of someone you already know. It could be an ex-partner, a friend, work colleague or someone you've already dated. During my time online I have come across at least a dozen people I know in this manner. What is the protocol in this situation? The respectful action is to move on. It may seem creepy or embarrassing to try and match with them if you have no intention of dating, even if it is just to say hello. Do not make the mistake of thinking that because you think it is OK, that they will too.

15. Manage Your Entry

Internet dating, as well as being a place populated by amazing people, is also a landscape full of rejection, abuse, deceit and cruelty. This can be a traumatising experience, especially for women and minorities. If not managed well, it can corrode you in a matter of days, leaving you feeling cynical, depressed, anxious, lonely and more full of hopelessness than before. It is critical therefore to manage your access. Just as many parents are concerned about how much screen time their children are exposed to, the same check needs to be placed upon ourselves when it comes to interacting with dating apps, especially when considered in conjunction with the daily use of our devices for other purposes.

The apps companies recommend 30 minutes use per day. **I would also suggest taking regular breaks to rest and be free of constantly checking your mobile for messages. When I first signed up I didn't do this, and after two or three weeks of full-on engagement I grew tired of constantly being switched on, like a sentry on duty. Being active every day means being perpetually vigilant, which I found mentally exhausting. Be as strict as you can in creating your own rest schedule. If you** pay a monthly subscription to any dating apps one good idea is to take a break each time it expires, which will also save you money. If you do this, ensure the auto-renewal is turned off within the settings on your mobile, otherwise you will be charged again. Alternatively, you could simply restrict your usage to Sunday's and Monday's only, which are the peak periods. On *Tinder*, most weekday activity takes place at 9am and 6pm, as people commute to and from work, and tails off after 9pm. This more episodic approach will offer a gentler learning curve than signing up for continuous exposure, and crashing headlong into the fray. The first time may be horrible, but the second time will be less so, and by the third, you may handle it better, and importantly, know what to expect. If you stay engaged long enough to acclimatise, the negative impact will begin to dissipate, until you get to the point where, as the saying goes, "it gets easier", and you are able to shake off the emotional shrapnel. Remember, *if you open the pipe, you get sewage* — but if you open it a little bit, you'll get a lot less.

16. Accept Rejection

It is hard for many to accept that online dating means that people will ignore and reject you. It challenges your notion of yourself as a desirable person who wants and deserves the best. But being ignored and rejected are daily occurrences you must accept with grace. *Everyone has the right not to love you, not to want you*, regardless of what you may think of yourself. Even if you decide to treat every dater respectfully, to not be nasty, to respond in kind to all messages, and to avoid ghosting people, others may still do these things to you. The best way to deal with rejection is to expect it. If you expect to be turned down, you can't be hurt. You should *expect to be nobody's first choice.* Then, if anybody does contact you, treat it as a lovely surprise, and be grateful. Be aware that this is not the same as having low self-esteem. Your self-esteem can be high, while still expecting to be rejected by those who don't think you are right for them, or who do not recognise your amazing qualities. Unfortunately, many of us are not yet in the position of acceptance, and so the whole experience leaves us doubting ourselves. Remember what my therapist once said to me:

> *Do not let the opinion of someone who has hurt you deeply, diminish your sense of yourself.*

17. Check Your Own Arsehole

The protocols mentioned in this chapter, as well as offering procedural guidelines, also represent the behaviours that online daters complain about the most. But one thing they often forget is that *they have probably done these same things to others.* In the world of online dating, everything is cyclical, and whether we realise it or not, we all have an active role to play in determining whether the apps turn out to be good, bad or ugly. Do not complain about being ghosted if you have ghosted people yourself; do not complain about being benched, if you have benched people too. Do not complain about daters losing focus because they are running multiples, when you are running multiples too. Before you judge how much of an arsehole everybody else is, address your own arsehole first. Or, as Mahatma Gandhi once said more eloquently; "Be the change that you want to see in the world."

10

WD-40

Thus far, the history of social apps has been dominated by young white males who have created their products to suit their own prerogatives. The shortcomings of a world designed by men for men is increasingly being brought to light, led by British author and feminist, Caroline Criado Perez, and her award-winning book, *Invisible Women*. Within the online dating arena *Tinder*'s face-body focus was conceived for the male gaze, with female users shoehorning themselves into a system not crafted to their needs. Even *Tinder*'s place-holder graphic — the default illustration used whenever a person chooses not to upload a photo — is male throughout, whether you are a male or female account holder. It is hard to imagine that had the app been created by a more diverse team, that things would be the way they are presently. Would they have been happy creating a product that encouraged users not to say anything about themselves, thereby avoiding being humorous, intelligent, emotional, truthful — and therefore human? Perhaps a group of female founders would have used artificial intelligence, not to predict what matches they think might work for us, which is its current focus, but instead to identify and remove dick pics, and then to ban offenders, as opposed to the current protocol, which relies upon women to report incidences *after* they have happened, when the damage has already been done.

Even though single people are rapidly conceding and accepting that Internet dating is both the present and the future, and that we have little choice but to participate or risk being alone, at present it is not an experience most people enjoy. A 2018 BBC study of 2,000 people reported that 37 per cent of 16 to 34-year-olds stated that dating apps are their least preferred method of meeting a new partner. The apps have a long way to go in terms of improving the user experience, the quality and relevance of the matches, in dealing with abusers and in protecting vulnerable groups such as women and minorities. Daters also need more guidance and encouragement to create better and more informative profiles, so that the apps work better for all. Time and time again they make basic mistakes in creating their profiles. When they sign up, the apps do not tell them about best practices, such as to smile in photos, not to wear sunglasses or post images of children. Judging by the overwhelming proliferation of these errors within people's profiles, many clearly do not know, and so their postings are sub-optimal. All the dating apps have guidelines about best practices somewhere within their websites — rather than within the apps themselves — and so users miss them and sign up without reading anything.

One improvement to the way things currently stand would be to downgrade partially completed profiles or those devoid of text within search results. People would be more incentivised to draft a written summary if they realised that no one would see their profile otherwise. Alternatively, sites like *Tinder* could improve the user experience by allowing users to filter out all profiles that contain no text, so daters can connect directly to those with something to say. These are the kinds of features that should be available to subscribers for the money they pay, but so far the app owners do not appear to be listening.

Instead of incorporating best practice guidelines within the apps, what we are offered is a huge volume of choice as a major selling point, whereas in reality this is more of a nightmare. In a world in which sheer volumes of every commodity are now out of control, choice has become useless as a selling point — whether we are on Amazon choosing a pair of shoes, or surfing a dating app. What we all yearn for is a curated solution — something that will just tell us the three best cheeses, the three best films on *Netflix*, and the three best candidates to date. In fact, humans have become so terrible at identifying who they should date that the apps are now attempting to use AI to do the job for us, thereby allowing us to bypass all the mush that is so damaging to the user experience. *Hinge* already offers such a system. But right now machines are clueless at selecting those we might find romantically attractive. The problem they have, and will always have, is that there is no equation for what humans call "vibe", "spark", "chemistry", or whatever it is we feel when we connect with that special person. There is no algorithm for matters of the heart. Despite the digital age, there are still some jobs left that only humans can do.

Others are convinced that the next tech wave in online dating will be augmented and virtual reality. "Imagine scanning people with your phone in a nightclub and seeing how many have made their dating profiles available," says *happn*'s Claire Certain. It is hard to see how such innovations will actually improve the user experience, as opposed to simply making it more visually interesting. Instead of making the graphics better, perhaps the developers should be offering free in-app courses in subjects such as, *How To Heal From Your*

Previous Relationship (Before Going Online). Ultimately, what the dating apps lack most is better information about its participants — and interestingly, this solution is retro, and doesn't rely on flashy graphics or technological innovations, but on people being more open and less afraid. And herein lies the problem — the app developers cannot design human behaviour. While the plethora of available dating apps may make nominal revisions to their graphics or features, the raw material they rely upon — the humans who populate them — will not necessarily revise themselves in tandem.

Despite the plethora of problems afflicting dating apps, major improvements to the current crop are unlikely to happen. While their marketing promotes the idea that their primary objective is to help us all find true love and live happily ever after, in fact, *failure is the business model*, just as it is in other industries founded on human fallibility, such as gambling or dentistry. Think about it like this — what would happen to the police force if there was no more crime in the world? Thousands would lose their jobs. So, while the police don't mind a reduction in crime, what they don't want is for there to be no crime. Dating apps are similar. They don't mind if a few people find love, but they don't want everybody to do so. Generally, they want us to *not find a partner* for as long as possible, because that is how they make their money, via subscriptions and in-app purchases. (Many female daters do not realise that men have to pay to connect with them, plus additional sums for special features). The apps first duty is not to lonely singletons looking for love, but to their company shareholders. Therefore, what is their incentive for making their apps better? Better apps means better matches, which means more people leaving. Their ultimate goal is to stop

161

people leaving — at least for a while. The apps are designed to create chaos, rather than order. It is precisely the fact that customers have to wade unsuccessfully through the endless mush that makes the business so lucrative for the app owners. Analysts predict that the global dating app market will be worth $12 billion by 2020. Match Group, which owns all the major platforms, has a market capitalisation of $2.3 billion. In 2018 it generated its biggest ever profit — nearly $500 million.

If anything, the financial success of the industry is predicated on sex, not love — because if we find love, we leave, whereas if we (mainly men) perpetually seek hook-ups and one-night-stands, we stay. The people are the product, and so the companies need us to continually re-subscribe at all costs. One way for them to retain our patronage is simply to buy up their rivals. Match Group, the industry's dominant force, owns *Tinder*, *OkCupid*, *PlentyOfFish*, *Match*, *Hinge* and *BlackPeopleMeet*. In 2017 they also tried unsuccessfully to acquire *Bumble*. In each case what Match Group are purchasing is not simply the data and intellectual property that each business holds — it is its customer base. A disgruntled *Tinder* user for example, who switches to *Hinge*, thinks they are leaving one app for another, when in reality they are simply moving to a different department within the same company. Another method app owners are using to retain customers is by expanding their offering to allow people to use their platforms as places to meet friends or business connects, as well as to date. Consequently, the apps have now repositioned themselves as "social" rather than dating platforms. In 2019 Whitney Wolfe, CEO of *Bumble*, announced on CNBC that her company "is not a dating platform anymore, it is a connections platform." *Tinder* is also mutating from dating into an entertainment app.

In order to appeal to its core of 18-25-year-olds, it has just introduced *Swipe Night*, an interactive game in which users navigate an impending apocalypse on Earth, with matches then tailored to the decisions players make within the game itself.

These new ways of trying to persuade users not to leave come on the back of the fact that there is still no hard evidence that the apps actually work in forging long-term relationships for the majority of users. Tim MacGougan, Chief Product Officer at *Hinge*, confesses that, "81 percent of *Hinge* users reported that they had never found a long-term relationship through a swiping app." In the recent HBO dating documentary, *Swiped*, when asked how many people who met on *Tinder* got married or ended up in committed relationships, Jessica Carbino, their in-house sociologist replied, "we do not have that information available." All she could offer was the anecdotal claim that she had been "inundated with emails" from *Tinder* users who had got married and had babies. The lack of convincing data suggests that the apps still have a long way to go in providing an effective love-matching service for their millions of lonely customers, and that the market may still have room for more workable alternatives. These alternatives are now on their way. In 2019 Facebook announced the launch of *Facebook Dating*. This may be good for the industry, if only to prevent Match Group from establishing a monopoly. And with Facebook now engaged, how long before Apple and Google enter? With these behemoths potentially looming, the existing dating apps will have to up their game, and make much needed improvements to their offerings if they are to survive in what is a transient and fickle market.

The efforts of the online dating platforms to provide convincing statistical data to persuade us to use and retain their products is a recurring focus. They replicate trends established in the food and beverage industry, in which they publish their own in-house research into their products in order to counter the negative findings of independent studies. In the era of fake news and "alternative facts" dating app owners tend not to hire independent marketing specialists to do their research for them, due to the risk that their conclusions may not all be favourable. Instead, they cherry pick the data and carefully control the design of the research in order to showcase only positive findings, which are then used within their PR and marketing to control the message about online dating. By contrast, independent research conducted by universities and media bodies routinely differs in design and results — often reaching more negative conclusions on many of the same data points. So whose research is to be believed — the online dating companies or the independent researchers?

However, it must be said that in the cases when dating apps actually do work in facilitating love between couples, the results are even better than they are with relationships formed offline in the old fashioned way. People who meet and fall in love via the Internet progress to marriage faster than those who meet offline, while research suggests that online dating has created more interracial and inter-faith relationships. This is particularly true in the United States, where the size and diversity of ethnic groups is bigger than in European countries. Online daters tend to be younger, and so this is where the shift is happening, as this group tend to be less set in their ways and more open to diversity. According to US census data, 10 per cent of heterosexual married couples in 2010 had partners of a different race or ethnicity — more than ever before — while the figure is 18 per cent for unmarried heterosexual couples.

These numbers may still seem small, but it is the speed at which they are changing in relation to the presence of online dating that is significant. Even though there is no doubt that we still live in a racially polarised world, things are steadily shifting nonetheless.

But for many single people it is emotional recovery, rather than dating or finding love, that is the primary objective of the apps. Despite the fact that they were designed for those who intended to meet, either for sex or relationships, we are now witnessing the effects of people using them instead to boost their self-esteem or to assist their recovery from past relationships — not by actually meeting people, but by *mining their digital attention*. When such adapted uses go well they can be of great benefit in helping the emotionally wounded feel better — but when they go wrong the results can be psychologically damaging. According to a study by America's National Academy of Sciences, the same areas of the brain that are activated when we experience physical pain are also triggered when we experience rejection. Meanwhile, a 2015 in-house survey of *Hinge* users found that 54 per cent reported "feeling lonely" after swiping. Like any potentially dangerous commodity, perhaps all dating apps should now be issued with a government health warning, like we have with cigarettes. Or further, they should be nationalised, and re-classified alongside other basic utilities such as water and power. The emotional state of a country's citizens, and the numbers who are or are not in loving relationships, should be of primary interest to all governments, as it directly impacts the wellbeing of nations and the costs of health and social care, crime and so on.

In the meantime, the apps, like social platforms in general, have facilitated a world in which many seek validation, not once in a while, but *several times per day*. Its users crave the constant sustenance of being narcissistically affirmed. It is the same obsessive behaviour characteristic of drug addicts. But for every day a person spends on the apps, feeling refreshed by those that like them, they simultaneously risk being corroded by those who do not. At any moment they may suddenly find themselves benched or brutally ghosted. It's like being kissed and then slapped afterwards. This is magnified by the fact that Internet daters expose themselves to more rejection than they would in real life. In the analogue world, being turned down by someone you met at a party or in a bar was manageable because it was limited in scope, but online you can be rejected or abused *dozens of times every day*. A week spent online dating can deliver more rejection than you would normally experience in a lifetime offline. This is the unregulated danger of digital culture — the dosages of everything are much higher.

Whether single people are using dating apps to recover or to find love, it is female users who are most vulnerable online. A 2017 survey by the Pew Research Centre revealed that 21 per cent of females between 18 and 29 have experienced sexual harassment online, with 83 per cent claiming online harassment to be a serious problem. Much of this is played out within dating apps. On *Tinder*, overwhelmingly, the single sentence I see women write the most within UK profiles is, "No ONS or hook-ups". This group are typically divorced, working, and with children at home, and so they tend not to be looking for casual sex. Their intention — to find a long-term, loving relationship — is at odds with the site's relentless male sex pests. As a result, many women have taken to expressing their displeasure by posting angry statements directed at these men, and which allude to unpleasant experiences they have been subjected to along the way. This is a fundamental problem with dating app design — people with different intentions, instead of being kept apart, are thrown together. This organised chaos may be great for business, but it is bad for those seeking relationships.

For women, part of this degraded user experience manifests in having to endure receiving dick pics from abusive males. A 2018 YouGov poll found that four-in-10 women aged 18 to 36 have been sent an unsolicited photograph of a penis. One wonders, what kind of response are these male abusers hoping to get from the women they are sending these genital selfies to? *Oh, hi there, I just received your wonderful dick pic. Such a gift! It was so thoughtful of you to send it, I am very grateful, in fact honoured, to have been chosen to receive such a beautiful specimen. Would you like to come over tonight, and we can put it to good use?*

The so-called crisis in masculinity has led us to the point where, for certain dysfunctional males, communicating through their genitals is all they can muster. The art of conversation has evaporated as they offer up their cocks instead of their brains. If the social convention of talking first and having sex later is regarded as a feminine trait, then it is this female side of masculinity that is missing here. Or if it is not missing, it is certainly detached, because hating women, if that is what this is, is also about hating oneself, because man is *of woman*.

Abusive male behaviour within online dating may be read as part of what British artist Grayson Perry refers to as, "rogue masculinity" in his book, *Descent Of Man*. It is connected to the wider challenges men are facing within society, as they lose their traditional power positions and become more disillusioned with their demoted place in the world. Not only is the #MeToo movement challenging established male prerogatives, but women are also now outperforming men both educationally and professionally. Female university graduates already outnumber men in many countries, while in the UK women are a third more likely to go to university than men. Many men are struggling to come to terms with the changeover, and within the online dating sphere, which is packed with professional women, connecting with those who may be more successful and more solvent than they are, and who are ready to make the first move on apps like *Bumble*, is breeding insecurities and resentments amongst many males. The new confidence of these autonomous females is further illustrated by their more proactive attitude to failing relationships. A 2017 survey of 4,000 Americans by sociologists at Stanford University and the University of New Mexico, reported that 80 per cent of divorces are now instigated by women.

But the main reason why incidences of male abuse within online dating are so high may simply be due to the massive gender imbalance amongst dating app users in different countries. The percentage of females on dating apps "never goes above 35 per cent", says Jean Meyer, founder and chief executive of *Once*. A 2018 study of 12 million mobile users across the UK, US, France, Spain and Italy, by mobile marketing firm Ogury, revealed that 85 per cent of the UK's dating app user base is male, while in the US the figure is 73 per cent. The report claimed that *Tinder*'s figures are even higher, with roughly *one female user for every nine male users*. In Italy, 91 per cent of dating app users are male. This kind of ratio occurs even with bespoke female-friendly app, *Bumble*, whose user base was reported to be 80 per cent male. Such massive discrepancies between the genders is partly explained by the fact that many male users are in fact not single. With men outnumbering women to such a large degree, it stands to reason there would be concurrently higher levels of abusive behaviour from that particular group. Put simply, more men means more abuse.

The result of all this is that being online as a man is a safer and more pleasurable experience than it is if you are a woman. Females often end up being more scarred by their online experiences, particularly black women, who are least favoured and sustain most abuse. Many cancel their dating app accounts in dismay, surrendering the landscape to the abusers, while the app owners struggle in vain to play catch-up. What is clear is that there is a marked and consistent behavioural difference between the sexes online. In short, women tend to be nicer. They generally do not send men photos of their vaginas as an introduction to a possible meeting. Trolling also, as seen across *Twitter* and other social networks, is defined almost exclusively by gender, consisting mainly of men being disrespectful towards women, with a minority of incidents perpetrated by females. It illustrates just how far men still have to go in terms of improving their behaviour and rising above being abusive toward the women they seek some form of connection with. There is much talk of the change being centred around men having greater respect for women — but this should not be the direct objective. If men had greater respect for themselves and their gender, then respect for women would follow naturally, as would world peace and the end of war.

The failure of dating apps to protect women from abusers is symptomatic of the apathy of society's gender-biased lawmakers. Many governments are still discussing whether or not sending dick pics — the digital equivalent of indecent exposure — should be criminalised, but right now, talking seems to be all they are doing. In the absence of government action, the apps should take the lead. *Bumble*'s Whitney Wolfe has taken up this mantle, and has been very pro-active in promoting legislation to criminalise the practice in America, but other dating app bosses have remained silent. In 2013 some dating app providers got together to form the Online Dating Association, a UK-based trade body which oversees standards and interfaces directly with app owners, regulators and law enforcement. Although membership is open to service providers globally, at the time of writing this, none of the major sites had joined, aside from *Match* and *Guardian Soulmates*.

But on a day-to-day level it falls upon the apps users to develop their own counter-measures. Ultimately there is nothing a female dater can do to address the bad behaviour of abusive men — except first to report it to the service provider, and then to *detach from it*. It can only hurt you if you let it. In order to date successfully online, women have to refuse to let abusers puncture their psyche or drive them away from the platforms, thereby surrendering the landscape that should be partly theirs to a few misguided fools. Granted, being resilient is easier said than done, as many women do not have the emotional armour to deflect such negativity, but the aim is to evolve an online practice which is *light-footed* — the objective of which is to skip away from trouble rather than to get bogged down in the swamp.

Despite the figures that reveal that Internet dating has now reached critical mass, with more single people meeting online than off, not everyone will be able to adapt to this new reality. Women who have suffered physical or sexual abuse at the hands of online daters for example, or those prone to severe anxiety, or others who are too emotionally sensitive to navigate its difficulties, are just some of the social groups who may be left out of the switch to digital. And what about professionally unsuccessful men with no money, who consider themselves failures and are racked with low self-esteem? The potential consequences for them are serious — they face a future in which they may be perpetually single, perhaps for the rest of their lives. Loneliness, or indeed being alone as a way of life, is now as big a trend as online dating. According to 2017 figures published by *Eurostat*, 34 per cent of people within the European Union live in single-person households, up from 31 per cent in 2010. Sweden tops the chart, with 51 per cent, followed by Denmark at 44 per cent. Large numbers of these people are single, perhaps disillusioned with relationships or unable to adapt to its new rules, and therefore they drop off the dating merry-go-round completely. It seems as if today we all have friends or know of individuals who are long-term single. I personally know eight people, mostly women, who have been without a partner for five years or more. According to a 2017 survey by sociologists at Stanford University and the University of New Mexico, over 80 per cent of single heterosexual men and women in America *did not go on a single date or hook-up in the preceding 12 months.* "The viability of singlehood as a permanent or semi-permanent adult status has increased over time as the age at first marriage has increased, and as interest in remarriage has declined," says Michael Rosenfeld, who led the research.

Part of what Rosenfeld implies here is that there is a whole generation of people who, following a difficult or traumatic break-up, bereavement or other event remain *unrepaired*. The women become boyfriend-proof, the men become girlfriend-proof. Now though, some pro-active singletons are seeking help. The biggest growth area within dating culture comes in the form of dating and relationship coaches and therapists who offer their services to singletons keen to acquire an emotional makeover and to learn how to navigate the choppy waters of digital romance. So far most of the takers are middle class single white females — the kind who may already be fans of psychotherapy, and who can afford to pay for specialist help.

For other single people, the action point may not be to seek help to change and find a partner, but instead to simply see Internet dating as a global chat room they use to combat loneliness, perhaps indefinitely. The future of dating may be about swipe-voyeurism and texting, rather than actual physical interactions and marriages, which are more difficult and require more effort. People are somehow *finding a sense of fulfilment in not meeting.* "It is easy now to meet people from your bedroom in your sweatpants, which makes things a lot easier," *Vogue* columnist and TV host Karley Sciortino told *VICE.* "It is also cheaper, because you don't have to go out to meet people." The implication here is that the experience of interacting with someone online has now almost become the equivalent of *actually meeting them* — despite the fact that you are not. Digital courtship has become an avatar for real relationships, and one that is condensed and accelerated into minutes or days rather than years. Two people interact on a dating app, where they say hello and then goodbye after just a few text exchanges; and this brief interchange is enough for people to go through the motions of a real life relationship, to feel hurt or betrayed by things the other person has said. The mechanics of meeting someone and then breaking up, which used to only happen physically, now happen virtually too.

These rapid and cyclical interchanges can make people feel as if they are going through an actual break-up, or a series of rapid break-ups, all with strangers they have never even met, spoken to, kissed or had sex with. In a bizarre twist, people now log off dating apps in order to recover from bad online relationships, in the same way that they once logged on to recover from offline relationships.

*

We are clearly not yet at the place where dating apps are serving the needs of those in search of loving long-term relationships. Other intentions — such as finding sex, countering feelings of loneliness or boosting ones self-esteem via the attention of admirers — are better catered for. The next generation of apps will have to adopt a different approach if they are to help facilitate the fulfilling partnerships that so many of us yearn for, and in greater numbers than currently occur. For me, the next logical step is to take all my observations and guidelines about online dating and to launch my own app that puts my ideas into practice. I will be working on this challenge in the very near future, so stay tuned.

However, despite the failings of the current options, my time Internet dating has been an incredible journey — from crying in the street over my break-up, right through to meeting new people and listening to the stories of their lives. Everybody I met was fascinating in a different way. Some dates were uncomfortable, others were horrible, and some were totally amazing. Some of those I dated have become good friends. One of the key takeaways for me, and that has nothing directly to do with my search for romance, may be summarised via these questions; *Am I now a more experienced person? Am I wiser and more emotionally nourished by connecting with other human beings who may be as flawed as me, or more so?* The answer is a resounding yes.

I am also happy to report that since writing this book I have found romance on one of the dating apps. She is a 47-year-old Englishwoman, and like me, she works in the media. She messaged me first on the app, but when I looked at her profile I saw that her attractiveness was obscured by her choice of pictures. There were only three, and in her opening shot she was looking down with her eyes averted, as if she was shy, afraid or insecure about something. But the sense of vanity and narcissism so characteristic of many online profiles was absent from hers, and this stood out for me. There were no mirror selfies or images of her in tight or flesh-revealing clothing. Pleasingly, her written text contradicted her photos — she was honest and open, and we seemed to like the same things — film, podcasts, books, Radio 4, running, Premier League football, red wine and cheese — *result!* Her A&L was also a fit. She lives just five miles from me in London, has two children in their late teens who don't need surrogate parenting, and are close to leaving home, plus an ex-husband who is not causing trouble in the background. Emotionally and physically she is ready and available.

She was so open in her bio that we met up very quickly, after just two or three exchanges. We went to a pub in the Holland Park area of West London, one Monday night at 7pm. I'd stated beforehand that I could only meet for an hour — a precaution just in case we didn't hit it off. I got there first and waited at a corner table with our drinks — red wine for me, vodka tonic for her. When she arrived we both frowned and studied each other for a silent moment, as if we'd met before. She asked if we had. "No doubt," I replied. "In another life or two." She raised her eyebrows and nodded as if that made complete sense to her. She was dressed unpretentiously, in jeans and a simple top, and the first thing that struck me about her were her deep-set eyes, which were ringed with shadow under the light, which gave them a certain intensity. She was nervous, and sat at the far end of our table rather than opposite me. But it didn't matter, because we both felt the same sense of relief and joy that we'd found each other, finally.

If it can work for me, it can for you. Consider the story of the Rocket Chemical Company, a firm which started life in 1953 in San Diego, California, with a mission to create a rust-prevention solvent and de-greaser for use in the aerospace industry. Working in a tiny laboratory with only three staff, they came up with a product we know today as the bestselling household lubricant, WD40. The "WD" in the title stands for Water Displacement, but what was more impressive was that the "40" referred to the number of attempts it took the founders to perfect its secret formula. I love this story because it is about persevering, about not giving up, about refusing to be derailed by setbacks, about refusing to be ground down. This is what all online daters need to do. Don't give up. Try again. Try smarter. The right person for you is out there — just not in plain sight.

Dictionary Of Online Dating Terms

Benching — keeping a dater on the sidelines without communicating.

Boyfriend-proof/Girlfriend-proof — someone who has been single for so long that they can't adjust to having a partner.

Breadcrumbing — restricting your chat to short, intermittent morsels, keeping the other person hungry.

Catfishing/Kittenfishing — to create an online profile with fabricated info, to attract more connects.

Firedooring — a dater who opens a dialogue, then ignores your response.

Flexing — showing off, bragging or boasting about yourself or your material possessions, within the photography, written profile or messaging.

Ghosting — to begin a dialogue, and then abruptly disappear without explanation.

Haunting/Zombieing — when a ghoster suddenly returns, back from the dead.

Hook-ups — getting together for casual, non-committal sex.

Love bombing — when a dater showers you in extreme affection and compliments early on in an effort to woo you, then cuts off, revealing their true, less appealing self.

Mirrorman/Mirrorwoman — a narcissist.

Running multiples — connecting, messaging with or dating several suitors simultaneously.

Skeleton — a dating profile that consists of a single photo, no text.

Slow fade — to gradually phase someone out by reducing the frequency of your chat, while lengthening your response times to their messages.

Yes/no — the state of emotional conflict between wanting a relationship and not wanting one.

Abbreviations

ONS — one-night-stand.

HNS/QNS — half-night-stand/quarter-night-stand. Like a one-night-stand, only the person leaves after the sex, without staying over.

FWB — friends with benefits.

NSA — no strings attached.

IRL — in real life. To go on a physical date with an online connection.

EU — emotionally unavailable. Someone who is psychologically blocked from being in a fully-committed relationship.

A&L — availability and logistics. A measurement of how much someone can devote to a relationship.

Also by Ben Arogundade — debut novel

The Sexual Language of Strangers

'A clever, dark drama.' Esquire

Ben Arogundade

Two illustrated titles on US presidents

Fake Views? The Donald Trump Book Of Covers
President Trump's rise to power, told through a selection
of his front covers, from 1979 to the present.
WINNER: General Non-Fiction: Indie Book Awards 2019.
FINALIST: Best Cover Design: Indie Book Awards 2019.

Obama: 101 Best Covers
President Obama's rise and two-terms in office, illustrated
via a selection of his covers, from 2004 to 2016.

All titles available at Amazon.

Ben Arogundade is a London-based writer, publisher and entrepreneur. His background spans architecture, graphic design and journalism. His first book, *Black Beauty* – an exploration of society's historical perceptions of the black image — was honoured by the New York Public Library and became the subject of a three-part BBC documentary. In 2016 Ben launched his own print-on-demand publishing imprint, White Labels Books, specialising in direct-to-consumer fiction and non-fiction.

Acknowledgments

Special thanks to Sue Amaradivakara, Natalia Cassel, Fiona Dent, Shreena Ghelani, Felicity Gray, Sarah Hirigoyen, Sophie Maunder, Kate Munro, Jane Partner, David Storey, Emily Stillman, Elvira Svanqvist, Sally Taylor and Emma Theander.

~~Try to~~ be your best self, online and off. Every day.

whitelabelsbooks.com

Printed in Great Britain
by Amazon